FORGOTTEN HERITAGE

Matthew Emmett

JONGLEZ PUBLISHING

Introduction

It was early, on a cold morning near the beginning of 2012, that we approached our first perimeter fence. The two of us crept slowly and quietly through the tangled undergrowth like ghosts drifting across the no-man's land of scrub that surrounded the huge industrial complex. Our camera bags snagged on low branches and our shoes squelched in the boggy ground. Up ahead, through the brambles and trees, the fence materialised out of the mist. We stopped, hunkered down and waited, scanning for any sign of movement. There was none.

We moved forwards again, stepping out moments later from the bushes onto the small grassy strip running alongside the fence. This outer fence was ten feet high and topped with three rows of barbed wire. It also bore two signs: 'Dangerous Site - Keep Out' and 'Trespassers Will Be Prosecuted'. Being a typical law abiding person, that moment by the fence filled me with a sense of dread and foreboding. Thoughts raced through my mind about what may happen to us if caught by one of the regular security patrols. Was it really a risk worth taking for the sake of a few photographs? But at the same time I was aware that for the majority of my life I had followed the rules, often blindly obeying with no thought as to why they existed. A mix of peer pressure and a sudden desire to do something 'a bit crazy for once' pushed me on. After passing my kit bag to my friend, I hooked my fingers into the interlocking links of the fence and began to climb.

All those who photograph abandoned locations, places classed as 'off limits' or on private land, are faced with this same dilemma each and every time they go out. If you want the shots then there is no place for second guessing consequences. You just have to go for it. Some locations are wide open and you can simply walk in; others are protected by layers of security. The prerequisites for access are a willingness to bend the rules, the ability to climb, move quietly, run quickly and an acceptance that you may get caught! Stories circulate of over-enthusiastic security guards with dogs, alarms that half deafen you and on the spot fines. Some stories are true and others are simply stories, half-truths invented to keep other people from diluting the originality of a photograph taken by only a handful of people.

For me and a steadily growing group of people from all walks of life and ages, infiltrating, exploring and photographing this myriad of fascinating and visually stunning abandoned structures has become an all-consuming obsession. There is an excitement and a thrill to be had in simply being somewhere the majority of society will not tread. The power these incredible spaces exert over us lies in the unique and special atmosphere residing within them. Take a vast abandoned power plant for example: once a noisy, frenetic place, full of the sounds of workers, the hum of power and the hiss of steam under pressure, now rendered totally silent, empty and still. It is this contrast between the before and after that gives them a beauty that cannot be found at world heritage sites or the managed pay-per-view houses and castles that litter the landscape. There is something truly special about not sharing a location with thousands of other tourists. It could be deemed selfish to want an atmospheric location all to yourself but, in a way, this is the same motivation that cave explorers or mountaineers experience. It is the desire to see things other people will not or cannot see for themselves.

From a photographer's point of view, there is a big advantage in shooting within the confines of an abandoned location: the stillness and silence allow you total focus on your surroundings and a visual aesthetic emerges that would have been much harder to define had the building been a busy, populated environment. In short, the building's character is laid bare.

I recently noticed a comment in response to an online article on abandoned photography. An architect had commented that 'architecture is designed with people in mind and that the true intended character of the building is only present when it is inhabited'. This may be so, but humans have transience coded into everything they do and create; we are constantly striving for progression and growth as if salvation somehow lies within, when certainly with regard to growth, the opposite is often true. Because of this need to progress ever onwards into a forward-facing future, our creations are destined to rise and subsequently fall as they become yesterday's bright ideas. For me the final weeks, months or years in a building's story are a part of its life cycle – as valid as the day it was built. To celebrate it visually is to pay homage to everything that has gone before.

Staircase within an abandoned Belgian house. A matter of weeks after I took this picture, the stair spindles were destroyed by vandals.

Legally, the hobby walks a fine line; being where you are technically not supposed to be puts you on the wrong side of civil trespass law. But provided you don't cause any damage or take anything away, then you remain on the right side of criminal law. If security personnel find you within a location, then you do as you are asked and leave without argument. Most people I have met through the hobby are very aware of the legal boundaries surrounding the shooting of abandoned buildings. They are respectful and careful as they explore each location. Metal thieves, rather than photographers, tend to be the most likely people harbouring negative intent, particularly in industrial locations. Only once did we come across a group of young men carrying camera gear who were also hard at work unscrewing light and door fittings before dropping them into a bag. It was quite a depressing sight.

The last four years have taken me across northern Europe and down as far as Italy, visiting rusting industrial remnants such as steel works, power stations, crumbling chateaux and every type of structure in between. The journey so far has enriched my senses, struck me speechless at the beauty of places left to rot and created memories I will never forget. It is a wonderful thing to have discovered a true purpose in life, something I knew straight away I could do well and, as it turned out, thanks to the Internet and social media, something that would also bring happiness to many others.

Sharing the discoveries from each location via social media is a positive and natural extension of the experience. Through photography, people who would be unable to access these places are able to see what lies beyond the boundaries. Reactions to the images have really turned what was already a very fulfilling hobby into something much more rounded and complete. Some people simply love looking through the images and experience strong emotional reactions to the sight of a once grand building gone to ruin. Others have a more personal connection in that they may have worked within the industry shown. And occasionally, some people are directly connected to a particular location. Hearing people's thoughts and reactions to these images turns what could be a fairly egocentric and solitary hobby into a two-way conversation, something of a shared experience. Visiting these places has been truly fascinating and a great privilege, but bringing them into the homes of so many others makes it much more worthwhile.

Sunlight cuts through the dusty atmosphere in an abandoned Belgian chateau.

Before we go on to the locations that make up the remaining chapters in this book, I would like to thank the many people who have supported me since I set up Forgotten Heritage. The words of encouragement and the enthusiasm with which people have embraced the photography and stories brought back from each trip have acted as great motivation to keep at it. I thank you all.

I would also like to say that I'm not a professional writer. However, it was very important that, in order for me to be true to the many people who follow my adventures, I write the copy for this book.

The following chapters will act as a walkthough for a wide variety of the locations that have captivated me over the last four years. Where a location is known in the public domain or has since been demolished, I will name it and give some history. If a location is currently in a ruined state and accessible, then precise location details would likely contribute to its further and often rapid destruction. It's a sad fact but there are people out there who would harm locations by either committing criminal damage or stealing items for personal gain. For these sites the description will focus on a personal account of my exploration. They are not in any particular order other than the next chapter being the first location I visited.

It's not quite the same as being there in person, but hopefully you'll agree that the images do a good job of representing the various vistas and special atmospheres that inhabit each building.

Exploring abandoned buildings is a risky activity that is potentially very dangerous: structural issues, falling debris, toxic chemicals, broken glass, nails and sharp objects underfoot and many other hazards can all be present. Depending on where you are in the world the legal implications can vary. Due to these inherent risks the activities highlighted in this book cannot be recommended or advised by the author or publisher.

www.forgottenheritage.co.uk
Instagram: forgottenheritage
Facebook: Forgotten Heritage
Twitter: @MattEmmett1

The skeletal remains of a barge at 'The Purton Hulks', Gloucestershire, UK.

Contents

Four NATO tropospheric scatter dishes lie discarded in a Lincolnshire field.

National Gas Turbine Establishment

Fleet, Hampshire, UK (Demolished)

Towards the end of 2011, a friend bought his first DSLR and asked me to show him the basics of photography. The first lesson took place in his back garden and when I asked if he found it useful, he thought that he might learn faster if we did the next one on location. A few weeks later, he came back with the suggestion that we climb the fence into a now derelict ex-Ministry of Defence complex. "It'll make for some interesting pictures," he said. I have already described in the introductory chapter the morning we first approached the National Gas Turbine Establishment (NGTE). Beyond its two layers of fencing were a series of hangar-sized structures: these housed what had been a highly secretive defence research establishment dealing with military jet engine development throughout the Cold War from 1950 to 2000.

Back in 1940, Frank Whittle and his company Power Jets developed the first British-made jet engine to power a plane in flight, the Gloster G.40. Over the next six years, during which time Whittle had great success developing his technology, the company was effectively taken from him through a process of nationalisation – this was due to years of heavy government investment. The company was merged with the gas turbine wing of the nearby Royal Aircraft Establishment, a location was found for this new company a few kilometres away from the RAE in Farnborough, and the National Gas Turbine Establishment in Fleet was born.

The Cell 3 supersonic jet nozzle and pressure bulkhead.

By this time, the Second World War had ended and the threat of the Luftwaffe had passed, but in its place a new potential enemy, the Soviet Union, had been growing in strength. The NGTE (or Pyestock, as it was also known) had became a focal point in the efforts to counter this threat. New planes with new capabilities were needed, able to outperform whatever the Russians were developing. This secret arms race was essentially the driving force in pushing forward British science and engineering know-how at an incredible pace.

During its lifespan, the NGTE was the leading institution of its kind in the world. Between its conception and the start of the next millennium, Pyestock was responsible for the design, testing and development of virtually all the UK's military fighter jet engines as well as naval gas turbine engines. Five pressure-sealed altitude test cells were built on-site to provide a testing environment for subsonic and supersonic flight. These closed-loop systems used compressed air generated in a vast turbine hall known as the "Air House". From this building, a mass of high-pressure pipes snaked outwards and across the site, which was the size of a town; the fast-moving airflow within could be redirected to any of these five testing environments – here it could be controlled to create simulated "air speeds", enabling the engines to be tested without leaving the ground. The Concorde project even had its own test cell on-site, "Cell 4". An extra power plant was built to accommodate this marvel of engineering, which was capable of flying the plane's Olympus 593 engines at Mach 2 and at a simulated cruising altitude of 57,000 feet (17,374 metres). Even with the Air House and the extra on-site power generation, Cell 4 engine tests could only be carried out at night due to the demand it placed on the national grid. People living nearby experienced the effects of the tests – house lights dimmed, images on TV screens shrank and a deep rumbling roar could be heard from up to several kilometres away.

The numerous buildings on-site all existed to provide an engine-testing function or an essential service for another building. In this way, the NGTE could be seen as a huge and incredibly complex machine. For testing to take place, everything had to run in unison, and the fact that it worked as well as it did was an incredible accomplishment. The work carried out there over its fifty years of operation placed Britain at the forefront of aerodynamics and gas-turbine engine development. Its legacy can be seen around the world every day by simply looking up at the vapour trails that criss-cross the skies.

Over time, new technologies such as computer simulations advanced to the point that they were able to accurately predict some of the data previously provided by physical testing. With the huge cost of running the site becoming hard to justify, it was gradually closed down in stages: the last staff left the site in 2000.

A short while after the close-down, the first of a growing number of photographers and urban explorers began infiltrating the site, eager to capture images of somewhere radically different to anything they had photographed before. They often climbed over the fences before sunrise to avoid detection by the security personnel who patrolled the site, then waited it out quietly inside one of the buildings for the sun to rise and the work to begin.

The view into the settling chamber of Cell 4, a dedicated testing environment for the Concorde project.

Angled shot for the Cell 3 jet nozzle and engine mounting rail.

On first entering the site, I was overwhelmed by its size and complexity, its palpable sense of place in Cold War history and the almost alien scenes that confronted me. It changed me instantly and I knew straight away that photographically this would become my focus. The main and most obvious attractions were the five engine test cells, although the site had a vast array of buildings – it would take many trips to see it all. During our first visit, we headed for the Air House, a huge building dominated by eight rows of machinery; each row featured one motor, one turbine and three compressor sets. This machinery was designed to generate phenomenal amounts of pressure: air was blown out of the east side of the building and sucked in on the west. The site's trademark blue pipes snaked outwards from either side of the building and delivered pressurised air to the nearby engine test cells.

Arriving at dawn inside this large industrial space was a spooky and magical experience; we were on edge and paranoid that security would burst in on us at any moment. The building made noises that convinced us there were other people in there too but, as time would tell, this was mostly rats in the ducting, pigeons roosting high above us or just the wind making the building creak. The Air House provided a great vantage point for photography: by climbing up a set of ladders and then moving carefully along an elevated rolling crane carriage positioned close to the roof, we could get a symmetrical pigeon's eye view of the entire hall and its repeating rows of machinery. From then on, we were prepared to take calculated risks to get the best angles for our shots.

After the turbine hall, we navigated north, using a simplified printout map of the site to reach engine test Cell 3. This particular cell was housed under a long shed-like construction that had another crane carriage – this had been used to load heavy jet engines into the testing tunnel. The tunnel itself was situated below ground level for noise reduction. As its lower-floor access doors had been welded shut years before, access was now only possible via the upper loading hatch in the roof of the tunnel.

The drop onto the metal gantries below was around 4-5 metres and looked far enough to cause serious injury should we fall. We found some old fire hose located in a nearby corridor and worked out a way of tying it to some sturdy pipework. We then spent some time arguing who would be the first to climb down; in the end, I opted to shimmy over the lip and slide down the hose into the gloom.

At one end of the cell was a circular array of vented openings arranged around a central jet nozzle – this was the business end of the cell and injected the high wind speed required to test military-grade jet engines at over Mach 1. When in use, the hatch covering could be winched into place and screwed closed, creating an airtight seal; air could then be sucked out of the cell via the vented openings to lower the air pressure and thus simulate high-altitude flight. Seeing it in the dim half-light cast from the hatch above was an awe-inspiring sight. It was like standing in the belly of some monstrous machine, the central nozzle like some great eye regarding us as intruders in its forbidden realm. The gantries on which we now stood were where the engines would have been bolted for testing to occur.

At the opposite end of the chamber was a set of futuristic doors that looked like something straight out of Hollywood … which is exactly what they were. The production crew for *Sahara* filmed at various spots across the site in 2003 and the doors were a leftover from one of the sets. Beyond this fibreglass construction, a smaller circular exhaust tunnel headed off into total darkness. Passing beyond the doors, I twisted the switch on the side of my helmet's LED lamp and flooded the tunnel with 1,500 lumens of light.

Part of the machinery that dehumidified the air before injecting it back into the closed loop system.

Decommissioned condenser in the sites large turbine hall.

Test Cell 4 seen from a lower angle.

The Air House or turbine hall generated a flow of high pressure air, required to power the nearby supersonic test cells.

Control panel by the Naval gas turbine testing tank. Ships engines were endurance tested here before being installed in the Royal Navy's ships.

After being abandoned for twelve years there were many parts of the site where damage was evident.

A short distance down the tunnel, a crude arrangement of strange metal rods could be seen protruding inwards from the tunnel walls. It was only afterwards, during post-trip research, that I discovered the rods were classed as inhibitor torches and would have had gas jetting out of them in a wall of flame that filled the tunnel. Their purpose was to combust any remaining traces of fuel that remained in the jet wash, thus preventing the risk of a build-up of highly flammable chemicals further along the test cell.

After taking lots of photographs, we managed to climb back out of the cell and found a subterranean service tunnel we had heard about that linked Cell 3 with Cell 4, located further north. Walking into this vast hangar-sized structure at ground level delivered one of the site's bigger "wow" moments. Towering above us, on our left as we entered, was one of the largest single bits of cast metal you would see outside of ship production. Cell 4 was built in 1965 as a dedicated engine-testing environment for the Concorde programme. In terms of sheer size and spectacle, Cell 4 was hard to beat. Being one of the main attractions, it was also one of the more obvious places to get caught by security, who would regularly enter the building, expecting to find photographers or metal thieves hard at work inside.

A tactic used by the security guards to try and locate us was to send one of their team along an air-intake pipe that used to supply the main airflow into the test cell. This terminated at an opening in the interior wall of the building about 6 metres above floor level. From a hidden vantage point, we once witnessed a member of the security team creep up to the edge of this opening, squat down and wait, listening for the sounds of people inside. Even the telltale "beep beep beep" of a camera timer was enough to bring them all suddenly bursting into the building, yelling at us to come out.

Outside the buildings, moving around the site was complicated by the ever-present threat that the infamous "Land Rover", or even someone on a bike or on foot, would round a corner and spot us. But usually, it wasn't too difficult to keep a low profile and remain on-site for the whole day. Certainly, if you were seen from a distance, it was simple enough to quickly move out of sight and then into a hiding place, where it was unlikely you would be found. The one and only time I got caught was on my final (eleventh) visit, when the "Land Rover" came round a corner without me hearing the few seconds of engine noise that allowed me to get out of sight. The driver pulled up alongside me and, with a rather confused expression, asked, "Are you supposed to be here?" As I was wearing a red helmet and attached lamp, I suppose I might have looked like a surveyor or an inspector. When I confessed that I was a photographer, we spent a while talking about his first week on the job and how he had been told that 99 per cent of the people he would come across would be photographers. On his first day, he had been shown the pictures taken of the site and posted online. After we had chatted for a while, he said, "I don't have an issue with people taking a few pictures. If you haven't seen me, then I haven't seen you, OK?" and I was then on my way again. Avoiding getting caught by the security team added an exciting element of cat and mouse to the often less adventurous activity of photography. The main reason people came, however, was to see a historic part of Britain's industrial heritage – something that only a few years before had been classed as a top-secret defence establishment.

My final trip took place just a few weeks before demolition began – I was on-site from late morning until nightfall. As it got almost too dark to shoot any further, I set up a shot of the iconic blue pipes, something I had neglected to do over the previous ten trips. As I shot my brackets, I said a fairly emotional goodbye to a place I had grown very attached to. After all the history and technologies developed there, and which have continued to revolutionise the world we live in, the National Gas Turbine Establishment deserved better than to be bulldozed into the ground.

Inside the Cell 4 settling chamber. Concorde's Olympus engines were tested in a capsule just beyond this chamber.

Cell 1 engine testing tunnel.
Built in 1957, it was the earliest
engine test cell on site.

Cell 4 seen from
the crane cab.

A view along
the hanger-sized structure
that housed Cell 4.

Inside the Cell 3 engine capsule. The doors shown are fibreglass, a leftover from the production of the 2005 film Sahara.

Abandoned House

Belgium

We visited this derelict house late in 2015 during the second of our twice-yearly trips to Europe. This particular trip resulted in us visiting a higher proportion of residential houses and farms than on previous trips. Having just moved on from the first rather disappointing location of the day (a much smaller and totally wrecked cottage), our hopes were high that the next, a larger town house, would deliver much more worth photographing.

After parking in a lane we made our way across fields towards the back of the house, doing our best to avoid being seen by anyone at the nearby farmers' market. Climbing over the fence into the field that bordered the overgrown back garden, I received a hefty jolt to my thigh from an electric fence and spent the first twenty minutes in the house nursing a sore muscle.

The chaos within the front room, drawers had been emptied onto the floors in what had obviously been a search for valuable items.

The rear aspect of this tall, thin building loomed skywards like a beanstalk. As we crept through the tangled back garden, a thick profusion of ivy and creepers hid any brickwork from view. The rear door was jammed open; on my right was a kitchen in complete chaos and on my left was a room shrouded in almost total darkness, the heavy foliage across the windows lending a dark green tinge to the gloom. A reasonably clear hallway passed by the main stairs and another doorway on the left opened into the living room, ahead of the nailed-shut front door.

Upstairs, the only rooms worth photographing were the front bedroom and the attic space. The rooms at the back on this floor were much too dark and dangerous to shoot in; the floors bowed downward under the weight of rotten wood.

The smell of damp hung heavily throughout the house and most of the walls were discoloured by algae and mould. Wearing dust masks we set up our gear and began working around each other, one room at a time, calling out when we had finished.

This house made a really interesting location to shoot because of the chaos inside. Drawers had been emptied onto floors in a way that made it look like it had been ransacked for anything of value, which is probably exactly what had happened.

Elements from shots I had seen previously were now missing, such as the large statuette of Christ that had sat on some drawers in the front bedroom. When a property is freely accessible like this, it is sadly inevitable that any items of value will quickly disappear. It is also sometimes the case that other photographers will hide key items to prevent others that follow from being able to get a similar shot.

Some rather rickety wooden steps from the first floor landing led up into the attic. A window at the front gave the only light into this dusty, cobweb-filled void. The back window was again covered by thick creepers. A collection of empty coffee jars at the edge of the attic caught my attention, but other than that, the space had little to recommend it.

After completing a tour of the house, one of our group did some further investigation and confirmed that the adjacent house was also derelict. Soon we were spread across the two properties. Next door had little worth shooting, but it's always worth opening all the doors to check. A rather atmospheric chandelier covered in cobwebs lay waiting in the attic.

Before we headed on to the next location we did a few exterior shots. The house had an unusually tall and narrow frontage with two sets of shutters, sagging symmetrically, each hanging on a single hinge. All in all it had been a big improvement from the first location.

A chandelier style light fitting was cast aside in the attic space of the second property. Covered in cobwebs it made for a wonderful subject in the soft light from the window.

A set of quirky and symmetrically wonky shutters on the front of the property.

The house frontage on a quiet unassuming Belgian street, surrounded by normal occupied properties.

A quirky statuette sits on the mantle, surrounded by the chaos of the living room.

A water pump in
the corner of the kitchen
and the sink full of debris.
This kitchen has not
seen a clean surface
in many years.

Abandoned Ethanol Distillery

Italy

When the company situated at this location first opened prior to World War II, it had been a busy industrial distillery producing ethanol-based products for various companies and industries, many of which were located close by. After World War II, the demand for production was greatly reduced due to heavy allied bombing across the entire region. The plant switched its focus to the production of alcohol for civil purposes (mainly the drinks industry), and by 1953, using ethanol fermentation to synthesise alcohol from sugar beets, it was producing over thirty percent of Italy's alcohol. The plant changed hands several times over the years but eventually closed in 2005 after an EU directive placed strict production quotas on Italy's refineries. It has been left at the mercy of the elements ever since.

A vertical panoramic image of the tower interior including its oculus style window.

In April 2015 we made the decision to travel further afield than our usual cross-channel trips to France and Belgium. We had seen some very promising images coming out of Italy from other photographers we knew. The country's architecture seemed to have a distinctive style. Add to it the crumbling stonework and faded patina that abandonment brings and the resulting mix is nothing short of magical.

The trip took in 14 locations across five days, with the morning of the third day taking us to a busy industrial district packed with canals, rail tracks and chimneys belching clouds of carbon dioxide into the clear, pre-dawn, turquoise sky. The perimeter wall that surrounded this derelict complex was a formidable barrier made from prefabricated concrete slabs. We had heard there was a breach in this wall but we were uncertain of its location and concerned the entire complex would take a considerable amount of time to navigate. However, as luck would have it, we made our way through the surrounding bushes and found the hole within twenty seconds.

Beyond the wall, the complex spread out across a large area: rusting chemical storage tanks, office blocks, laboratories, gantries, pipe runs and in the centre of it all a large circular tower. Making our way towards the tower, we were reminded to keep our wits about us as a deep hole in a metal walkway was soon discovered, partly covered over by long grass and creepers that had grown up in the years since the plant closed down. We also had no idea if there would be any on-site security patrols, so we moved swiftly and stealthily.

We had set an alarm in order to catch the sun breaking the horizon. The interior of the large tower was to be our main target: an imposing brutalist structure fabricated from massive sections of single cast concrete, dotted generously with windows around its circumference that provided spectacular views across the rest of the plant. Entering the tower on the ground floor, we were able to look up between the floors and see clear to the top of the building, its crane gantry and oculus-style roof lantern.

The sun was still just below the horizon as we made our way up the metal stairs linking each floor. On the third floor we broke out the tripods in anticipation of the coming light show. Getting good light can make a world of difference to the final shot – 'beautiful light' is one of the first things a photographer will notice in an image. But it has to be the right kind of light and there are only two short windows of opportunity: one hour just before dawn and an hour before dusk. The sun is not too high in the sky and the light reaching you has to travel through more of the earth's atmosphere, effectively filtering the light and changing its colour temperature to a warmer hue.

As dawn broke, the interior of the tower was transformed, the drab concrete structure reflecting pools of glowing light all around us. It is moments like this that elevate these locations, making them comparable, from an experience point of view, to many world heritage sites. It may not hold an important place in history or have been the scene of a famous historical event, but the fact that it's just you and the building allows you to connect with the environment in a way that is otherwise impossible.

We spent the next 60 minutes hurriedly shooting the tower from as many angles as we could. As the light grew harsher it was time to explore further afield. There was a fantastic view to be had from the roof of the tower; looking down on the collection of rusting chemical storage tanks that sat alongside made for some interesting close-up abstracts.

After the tower, we spread out across the site and discovered the fermentation vats and chemistry labs, but we did not have enough time to do it all justice. On these European trips, the next location usually entailed a drive of some distance, and to achieve the number of planned locations per day, calling time on a location was sometimes the only way to keep on schedule. As a result, the tower features in the majority of the images.

A view of the tower
from ground level.

The interior of the large industrial tower
at the center of the distillery.

A view down
onto the chemical
storage tanks, taken
from the roof of
the tower.

Abandoned Psychiatric Hospital
Italy

During a photographic trip to northern Italy in April 2015, I had the chance to visit a location that I had wanted to see for a long time. Having seen many photographs from inside this large, abandoned psychiatric hospital, I was struck with just how rich in fantastic imagery it was. Normally, a location yielding two or three high-quality images would be enough to justify the time spent travelling to see it. However, this one looked to be blessed with glorious features and vistas throughout, so a trip to this hospital was one of our main motivations for coming to Italy.

Constructed in 1871 in a figure-of-eight layout around two outdoor garden pavilions, the building has three floors and covers an internal area greater than 30,000 square metres. One half of the hospital was designed for male patients and the other for female. Each pavilion was an open garden space where the patients could spend time outside whilst being kept secure within the walls. In the centre of the structure, separating the two pavilions, was the medical wing. Clinical research and studies in the fields of pathology and radiology were carried out here by some of Italy's most respected doctors. There was also a dental suite, an electrotherapy suite and an operating room, all of which can still be found on the site. Exploring these facilities and knowing their tragic history made for a strange and unsettling experience. At its peak during the two World Wars, the hospital housed over 1,500 patients. The last inmates left in 1981, when the hospital finally closed its doors.

Patient records spill from wooden storage cupboards in an administration block within the asylum.

In the early 20th century, the hospital gained a specialist reputation for conducting some of Europe's first prefrontal lobe lobotomies on patients. The now discredited technique involved drilling two holes in the cranium, just above the eye sockets, and then inserting a metal "ice pick": this was scraped across the surface of the brain to sever nerve connections on the prefrontal cortex, an area of the brain that governs personality and social interaction. For patients suffering from severe mental illness, the procedure often had the effect of alleviating the more extreme aspects of their condition … but at a drastic cost to their personality, emotions and decision-making abilities. In many cases, violent and aggressive patients became more "manageable" for the hospital staff, but they were left with other lifelong problems. The outcome differed greatly from patient to patient, with some improving enough to be released from the asylum to continue life outside, although around 5 per cent of patients died during the procedure. Due to its controversial nature, the procedure had all but ceased by the mid-1950s.

On the day of our visit, we parked well away from the hospital walls and made our way across fields to arrive at the back gates of the hospital grounds. It was very early and only a few people were around, making things a lot easier for us. Stepping through a gap in the fence and into the compound, we emerged onto a tree-lined road that ran northwards through the site. We were surrounded by numerous derelict buildings, but we had only come to see the large main hospital at the far end of the site. After climbing a final set of gates that clanked loudly as we went up and over, we accessed the building via a basement. Next we went up a flight of stairs to emerge into a cloister corridor flanking one of the two open pavilions.

Being the only people within such an impressive abandoned and historic space, early in the morning, is a very special experience. Silence dominates and, apart from the scrape of our footfalls and the occasional sounds from the small Italian town waking up outside, the passage of time was marked only by a church bell clanging hourly from somewhere nearby. Knowing what had happened within these walls over the past 140 years made for a highly charged atmosphere. After a short group tour of the three floors, we all headed off in separate directions. We could hear the sounds of our tripods being unpacked and extended from the moment we separated.

Suddenly being alone in such a place is an exciting, but also an isolating and eerie experience. Nevertheless, it is important if you want to connect with the building and capture the best possible shots. I started on the top floor, shooting the crumbling patina and stunning light in shuttered corridors around several patient wards. Next I made my way into an attic space, where a rickety old ladder led to a high porthole window overlooking one of the garden pavilions. Finding unusual angles and shots not seen before at a popular location is a very satisfying part of photographing heritage sites.

Another part of the building that provides some fantastic imagery is within the administrative wing at the very front of the hospital. There are some floor-to-ceiling storage units, with wooden doors, in two adjacent rooms; one of the rooms has suffered fire damage and is blackened and charred. In the room without fire damage, what look like patient records litter the floor, spilling out of the cupboards. The diagnoses and treatments of the unfortunate inmates are on show for anyone able to read Italian. All across the asylum are clues to the great sadness that once filled these rooms and corridors: metal cages that held patients below a large hall; wooden gurneys with hand and foot straps; sinister-looking medical equipment that would look more at home in a torture dungeon …

Bars on the window secure one of the patient wings within the asylum. The many years of growth outside have covered the exterior of the building in foliage.

The view from an attic window looking across one of the garden pavilions. What were once small trees in the garden are now taller than the hospital itself.

The coexistence of such stunning beauty and a strong sense of sadness in locations such as asylums makes for perfect photographic conditions. The images strongly convey my feelings while I was there. Photography is such an important medium for conveying visual information, and even feeling and mood. This location ranks as one of the most atmospheric and interesting places I have explored to date.

I will end with an amusing story of something that happened to me while I was shooting in one of the asylum's exercise halls. I tend not to get too unnerved when alone in creepy places – I have experienced very little in the way of supernatural occurrences over the years. However, having just set up the tripod and spent a few moments composing the shot, I became aware, subconsciously at least, that a small bell had just rung out nearby. It wasn't until the second ring, a few moments later, that I became acutely aware of the sound – a definite "ding-a-ling" a short distance behind me.

I spun round, expecting to see one of my two companions but, apart from me, the hall was silent and empty. My hair stood on end and a shiver ran down my body from head to toe. I quietly crept around, looking for the origin of the sound – I had gone from non-believer to believer in a heartbeat! After nervously packing up my gear, I hurriedly left the hall and went in search of the others. I found them hard at work in the admin block. They looked both amused and concerned as I told them what had happened.

Four and a half hours after arriving at the hospital, we were back in the car, driving towards the next location, and there it was again: "ding-a-ling", the phantom bell rang out. One of my companions asked, "Was that the sound you heard?" Only then did I remember installing a new email app on my phone as we drove to the asylum. The bell was the sound of an email notification going off in my backpack. I had just never heard it before!

One of the upper floor corridors, near the patient dormitories.

Some of the equipment left behind in the medical wing of this large abandoned asylum.

*One of the now empty
rooms on the top floor
of the medical wing.*

One of the fire-damaged sections in the administration wing.

The Farm School

Waterloo, Belgium

This was a location we managed to squeeze in on our journey back through Belgium en route to our ferry home. We didn't have a lot of time but the location was only a short detour so we decided to give it a go.

After parking up in a residential street next to a large construction site, we made our way through the thick, churned-up mud towards a series of low-rise buildings. Inert diggers and construction equipment surrounded the structures threateningly – like a siege between the armies of the modern world and the old.

There has been a school here since the 1910, although due to the outbreak of the First World War the site was not populated with students until 1926. Architects Fernand Bodson and Théodore Clément designed the site as part of an alternative education campus for children who had problems integrating into mainstream schooling. It was created as part of a city garden project where children could learn various agricultural skills, such as crop planting and livestock management. The school was designed so that the work performed on site would also benefit the wider community. During the 1960s, a vocational training college and medical educational institute were added, providing the students with an even broader choice of vocational skills, such as basket making, carpentry, cobbling and tailoring. In 2007, the vocational skills part of the campus was relocated to a nearby technical college, spelling the end for the wider school. The site quickly fell into abandonment and dereliction.

The stunning infinity effect within the long corridor that remained standing at the center of the construction site.

Judging by the expansive field of mud around us, many of the outlying buildings of this once sprawling campus looked to have already been demolished. But in its centre was a long, narrow structure with small clusters of satellite buildings branching off its length.

After finding our way inside through an open window, we quickly realised why this section of the building had been left standing – it had effectively been saved from demolition by the beauty of this corridor stretching away into the distance. Although it is actually around 225 metres long, standing at one end and looking down its length gave the impression of an infinite tunnel.

A fine mosaic floor, a repeating series of arches and wall-mounted radiators added to its 'endless' effect. It was certainly one of the most beautiful corridors I have seen. Half way along its length, a small rectangular chamber divided the corridor. A wall in this chamber was decorated with a mural depicting various wetland birds. At the far end, a short corridor led off to a dilapidated gymnasium, its floor a dried carpet of pigeon guano. Despite the slightly faded interior, some impressive architectural details were still evident.

After only an hour here, we had to quickly pack up and head back to the car in order not to miss the ferry. The short visit to this fairly small location left a lasting impression on me, proof that great architecture has the power to radically affect our emotions in a positive way.

At the time of writing, the 'Bella Vita Project', a new development at the site, has been completed, converting the entire location into a retirement village. Fortunately, the corridor and gymnasium have been sympathetically incorporated into the design. It is nice to see such outstanding architecture being saved and reused in this way. Hopefully this beautiful corridor will continue to provide the site's new residents with much enjoyment for many years to come.

The central chamber with skylight half way along the corridor.

At one end of the corridor was this surviving gymnasium.

Abandoned Power Station and Steel Plant
Luxembourg

During a visit to a region in the far south of Luxembourg, we managed to visit two quite different locations that originally formed a large single industrial complex. All that now remained of the four blast furnaces that once towered over this town were several long warehouses once used to store the iron-rich soil after which the area is named.

Terres Rouge is situated right on the border of Luxembourg and France in the town of Esch-sur-Alzette. The area features many ruins of the once dominant industries that flourished here since the end of the 19th century. A short distance from these warehouses, across the open ground where the furnaces once stood, is the imposing ruin of a thermal power plant. Powered using by-product gases from the nearby furnaces, this symbiotic relationship worked well for the life span of the local steel industry. But as the supply of iron ore in the area began to run out, one by one the furnaces went cold. In 1997 the owner (Arbed) was forced to close the final furnace, thus also forcing closure on the thermal power station. Since being abandoned, both locations have fallen into a steady decline, becoming the haunt of local youth, graffiti artists, metal thieves and photographers.

Part of the external structure of the ore warehouses.

On arrival we visited the warehouses that formed storage areas for the unprocessed iron ore. Each huge building consisted of an upper floor full of deep bunkers where the earth was stored and a lower floor that has since flooded. It's a long space and walking around it feels pretty dangerous; the bunkers on the upper floor are deep and largely empty of earth now. The views from the smashed windows of this floor across to the distant power plant offer a sad vista – a landscape that once flourished but is now contaminated and dead. The lower, flooded section of the warehouse features the tapering bases of the bunkers hanging down from above, along with machinery that gravity-fed the ore into train hopper cars running on tracks directly below the bunkers. The tracks are now hidden from view by floodwater and submerged debris.

A lone building covered in graffiti stands close by, its purpose unknown. The only clues are the thick metal plates and deep holes set into the concrete floor where heavy machinery was once bolted down. It provided good views back to the ore warehouse through its shattered windows.

After we had finished at the iron ore warehouses, we drove around the fringes of the site and parked much closer to the power plant. Making our way over the fences towards the imposing structure, we passed a signalman's box – a remnant of the railway that used to pass through the site, bringing in raw materials for the furnaces.

Once inside the power plant, we were impressed by what we found. We had seen photographs but they didn't make it look particularly fantastic. The turbine hall was largely stripped out and wire casings were strewn across the floor; copper thieves had obviously been hard at work. I managed to find a small door on one of the mid levels that opened onto the high gantries running around the top of the turbine hall. It was from here that I accessed the rolling crane carriage to get an elevated vertorama of the entire hall. While I was taking the shot, a group of local schoolgirls in uniform came through the door and began sharing cigarettes on the gantry. Hiding out in a vast derelict power station while playing truant from school is one way not to be found. The people you come to share these spaces with when photographing can be quite varied, but schoolgirls were a first.

We spent around three hours inside the power plant and managed to see pretty much all of it. By the time this book is published the demolition of this structure will have begun.

Looking along the upper floor of the iron ore warehouse.
Following page: The ground floor of the warehouse is now flooded.

The ore warehouse, seen through the broken windows of a nearby structure.

Previous page: The view through the shattered windows of the warehouse to the distant ruins of the thermal power plant.

Some of the machinery within the thermal power plant.

The view along the turbine hall within the Terres Rouge power plant.

Stunning industrial symmetry on the upper floor of the power plant.

A staircase in a pool of light in a corner of the power plant.

Vehicle Graveyard

Southern Belgium

A European trip in the autumn of 2013 took us further south than any of our previous journeys. Headed for a series of mostly industrial locations in Luxembourg and France, we made our first stop in a small southern Belgian village close to the Luxembourg border. To our surprise, the village bore the same name as the location we were looking for: locations are usually given codenames to protect them from scrappers and vandals, but on this occasion someone's imagination had clearly run dry. We were here to see an extensive vehicle graveyard contained within three overgrown paddocks and scattered throughout the woods that surrounded them.

One of the many Mercedes Unimog trucks littered around the wooded site.

We picked a parking spot in a country lane that skirted the far side of the site then made our way back towards the main entrance along a boggy dirt track before branching off through thick stands of fir trees. We couldn't be sure which part of the site we were headed for or even if we would hit it. As doubt set in, a row of what looked to be the rear ends of jeeps suddenly emerged from the thick tangle of foliage. They were parked closely together and backed up against a barbed wire fence on the edge of one of the paddocks. Negotiating the fence and peering through one of the grime-encrusted windows revealed an interior filled with thick cobwebs and dirt. The passenger seat window had been left wound down and the undergrowth from outside had found its way in. They had clearly been parked here for a very long time.

Squeezing between the jeeps into the open paddock presented us with lots of options; the space was filled with a huge number of vehicles, including trailers, boats and trucks. This was going to be a very different few hours shooting to normal. Many of the vehicles in the paddock were of German origin: 'Hanomag' and 'Auto Union' were among the emblems emblazoned on bonnets. Some military-looking trucks were marked with the DDR logo, showing they had been property of the former East German state.

The grass and undergrowth that had been left unchecked in the paddock was wet after a recent shower and our trousers and shoes were quickly soaked through. We were aware from satellite views we had printed out that the house at the centre of the three paddocks was never far away, so everything was done quietly. Once you get down to the business of shooting, you descend into a solitary world, focused entirely on your surroundings, occasionally passing each other with a smile or a comment.

After taking shots of various vehicles being consumed by thick vegetation, I moved into a nearby wood and discovered rows of 'Unimog' trucks, a series of off-road vehicles manufactured by Mercedes-Benz since just after World War II. There were several peeking out of the edge of the wood, the cab windscreens and radiators clearing the thick vegetation. A lone 'Unimog' sat nearby under the trees on a bed of fallen autumn leaves. The shot I took of it set against this golden road is my favourite from this location.

After about two hours, we had a close call with a car being driven through the site. We ducked down and watched through a gap in some bushes as it flashed by some six metres away. We decided to call it a day shortly after that. On the way out I managed to climb in the back window of one of the jeeps we first encountered to get a shot of the steering column covered in cobwebs. To date this has been the only vehicle graveyard we have photographed but it remains a favourite.

A rusty trailer tucked away in a corner of the first paddock.

An auto Union jeep engulfed in undergrowth. Auto Union was a direct predecessor to Audi.

A Hanomag truck peeks out of the bushes. Hanomag was a Hanover-based manufacturer that also made military halftrack vehicles during the Second World War.

This truck of unknown make was pretty well camouflaged against the forest behind it.

Close-up on
the front grille of
an Auto Union jeep.

Inside the cobweb-filled cab of a Unimog Truck.

A Unimog truck sits on a golden bed of Autumn leaves.

Cooling Tower

Belgium

Certain locations quickly become favourites of the exploring/photographic community. Pictures emerge online of a strange, otherworldly place, its co-ordinates get passed around via email and, provided it's not located in some hard to reach spot, images quickly begin to flood social media channels and forums. As the internet becomes saturated with almost carbon copy images, the site falls victim to its own popularity and the visits decline. With time spent out of the spotlight, the location rises in popularity again and the cycle starts over. This location, despite being one of the Northern European classics, does not follow this cycle and has remained a hot favourite pretty much constantly. One reason for this could be that it is easily accessible, situated in a busy industrial town in central Belgium and provides an exciting and truly sensory experience.

The location is a large cooling tower next to a looming derelict power plant. A busy canal and lock separate the plant from the tower, with the services that pump the hot water to the tower crossing the canal on a dedicated bridge. The purpose of cooling towers is to cool and re-circulate water that is boiled to generate the steam that drives the turbines within the station. The water is pumped upwards to spray nozzles or into troughs that spread the supply across the full width of the tower. It then trickles down through a series of containers and drops into the pond. During its descent the water will have lost much of its heat through evaporation as steam. This then rises up and out of the top of the tower. Cooled water can then be pumped back to the power station to be reused.

A view of the platform, riser pipe opening and the condensing pond below.

Our first visit here came near the start of 2013; the town forms part of one of Belgium's industrial heartlands. Having passed through it on several occasions, we have noted the number of abandoned buildings that are dotted around the town and joked that we could spend a few weeks here shooting. Indeed it has earned itself the rather dubious title of 'Europe's most depressing town.'

As often happens when still fairly new to the hobby, we wasted a lot of time trying to gain access to the tower. A few workers from the scrapyard next door were watching us as we approached the perimeter fence around the tower. As we now know, most people simply do not care and we should have just carried on. Instead we backed off and took a torturous route through thick undergrowth to arrive unseen a few yards further along the lane. More stealth tactics followed at the base of the tower as we attempted to climb the steps leading up to the access door. A man and a dog were 'patrolling' the opposite bank of the canal so we waited patiently until he was looking away before one of us dashed up the steps. In retrospect, we all agreed that the man was most likely just out walking his dog!

We stepped through the door onto a platform elevated thirty feet above the mud and water of the condensing pond. The platform was formed by concrete walkways radiating from the centre like spokes. Between them, the remaining space was filled with cooling troughs. The platform's centre was dominated by a moss-covered opening that curved inwards and downwards, getting steeper until it became a vertical pipe. The atmosphere inside was unfamiliar and exciting – the perfect conditions for photography!

Entering the interior of the structure for the first time was a strangely uplifting yet disorientating experience. The vast cylindrical space with its strange angles and acoustics stretched upwards for a considerable distance in rows of concentric rings, its diameter narrowing as it went. At the top, a small disc of sky and clouds bathed the interior in a soft, diffused light. Adding to the surreal atmosphere of the space, the shrill screeches of two hawks nesting near the top echoed around the walls from time to time, and every foot scuff against concrete would crisply reflect. It was a total feast for the senses.

The three of us went to work, spreading out to avoid getting in each other's way. The scene covered such a wide field of view, both horizontally and vertically, I knew straight away that I would have to shoot panoramic images, or in this case vertoramas.

(Panoramic images are a series of images taken covering a wider view of the scene than your lens will allow, with the camera panned horizontally or vertically for each new shot, leaving a slight overlap with the previous shot. The overlap allows the images to be blended together either through dedicated image stitching software or by using blending techniques in Photoshop.)

After shooting a series of panoramic images on the platform it was time to head down below to get a shot from beneath the platform. Getting into position for the shot required entering the water briefly to pass under a low gap with only a narrow clearance above water level. Achieving this without falling in was tricky to say the least.

While I was setting up the shot I noticed the water surface swirling around me. A bubbly froth was forming in places and it looked as though the water level was rising! I got ready to grab the tripod and head out when I realised that it must have been due to the industrial lock situated on the canal next to the tower. As it purged water downstream the pond filled slightly with overflow from the canal.

The pictures I gained from my first trip to this tower were hugely popular online and were featured in numerous media articles. Photographers often credit certain images with raising their profile or helping them progress onto the next stage of their career; the cooling tower shots certainly gave me a big boost. I have since shot twice more at this location and enjoyed it equally as much as my first visit. Each time there were others sharing the space and being amazed by it. I have no doubt it will continue to attract visitors for many more years to come, or at least until the local authorities decide to demolish it.

In the humid interior of the tower, ferns find purchase in the cooling troughs.

Following page: A shot looking up at the underside of the platform from down in the mud and water of the condensing pond.

Close-up on the moss covered riser pipe opening in the center of the platform.

Following page (left): The exterior of the cooling tower.

Following page (right): Looking straight up and out of the tower.

The Royal Aircraft Establishment
Farnborough, UK

It was largely due to the repeated visits I made to my first location (a jet engine testing establishment in Fleet, Hampshire) that a trip to these historic, privately owned wind tunnels was made possible. I became aware of this location through discussions with people about the nearby National Gas Turbine Establishment. They assumed I was talking about the wind tunnels at Farnborough Airport, but when I researched online I realised there were, in fact, two sites located close together that both played pivotal roles in the early development of aviation.

The Farnborough wind tunnels were a precursor site to the NGTE and were designed with a much broader set of testing criteria: scale models of entire planes, wing and tail sections, bomb casings, missiles and other vehicles such as cars and boats could be tested for their aerodynamic properties. In the Low Speed (subsonic) 24' Tunnel within the Q121 building, entire prototype planes could be suspended within the airflow and tested for flightworthiness without endangering a test pilot's life.

Balance mechanism in the downstream end of the transonic tunnel's working section, housed within the R52 building.

There has been a military presence on the edge of what was Farnborough Common since the Army Balloon Factory was set up here in 1905. The importance of the site grew with the onset of World War I and the name was changed to the Royal Aircraft Factory. Experimental planes were built and tested before being put into service over the battlefields of northern France and Belgium. In 1917 the R52 building was built. It was the first of several that would house aerodynamic testing tunnels and the site was designated a key research location for new aircraft design. All manufacturing was taken off-site so that engineers could focus entirely on pushing forward Britain's knowledge in this emerging and specialised field. The change in focus brought about another change of name and the site became the Royal Aircraft Establishment (RAE). The RAE worked on numerous new aircraft designs, all highly secretive projects at the time, and many of the engineers who worked there went on to form companies that became household names, such as Rolls Royce and The DeHavilland Aircraft Company.

In the decades that followed, propulsion systems advanced from propeller-powered planes towards newer and faster jet engine technology. As the UK progressed into this 'Jet Age', the slower wind speeds generated by the RAE wind tunnels became insufficient. A new site was needed where much higher velocities could be reached for transonic and supersonic engine testing, so the National Gas Turbine Establishment, just down the road in Fleet, was formed.

Since then, the wind tunnels at Farnborough continued to play an important role in the field of aerodynamic research, although for the last thirty years the tunnels have been kept in an inactive state, locked away from public view. Only the Q121 tunnel is still classed as potentially operationally viable should the need to restart testing arise.

I made my first approach to the management company that looks after the wind tunnels back in January 2013. I presented a selection of images from the NGTE and requested access on the basis that I would be creating a comprehensive record of imagery of two historically important and linked sites. The company was open to the idea but, as always, things never go totally smoothly when it comes to permission visits to private locations. The site was about to undergo redevelopment and I would have to wait until its completion. Health and safety regulations looked as though they could also be problematic.

Communication continued until almost a year and a half later when an arts company took up residence within the tunnels and set up a series of audio-visual art installations. An opportunity to visit the tunnels appeared that satisfied the health and safety aspect of me needing to be supervised within the location, and both parties very kindly agreed to allow me to work around the exhibits, shooting the R52 and Q121 tunnels on two separate days.

The tunnels were everything I hoped they would be, a gold mine of photographic imagery and a very special and fascinating part of wartime history. This location has been one of many highlights for me from so many incredible places visited during the first four years of running Forgotten Heritage.

I would like to say a special thanks to both companies involved for making these trips possible.

The vast mahogany fan blades in the low speed wind tunnel within the Q121 building.

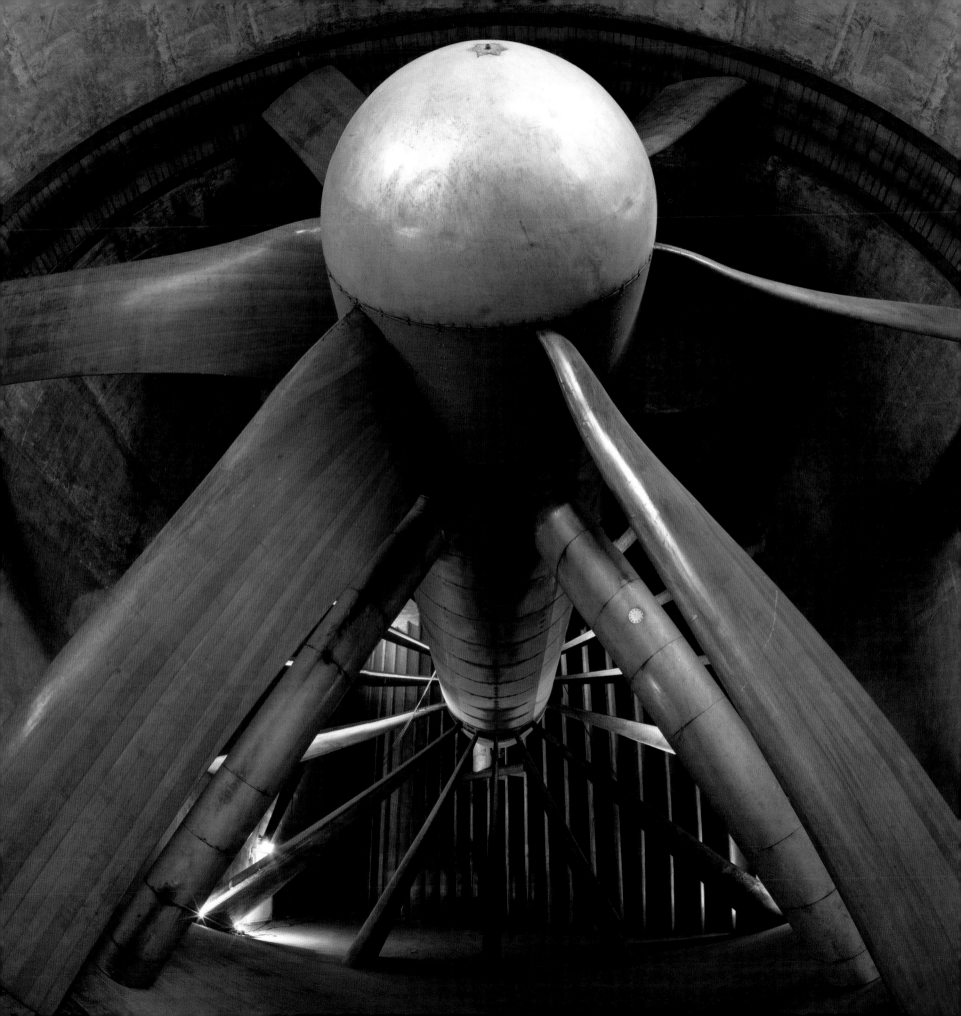

Within the main return in
the Q121 wind tunnel,
the four sets of vertical
blades carried the airflow
around the ninety-degree
turns before crossing the
testing platform and back
into the fan opening.

The sixteen air-straightening fins behind the main fan in the Q121 tunnel. The column of air coming off the fan was rotating and the fins helped to counteract this.

A propeller rig within
the Q121 building.

Warning
Fragile roof

FIRE EXIT

*Door to the engine room
that powered the Q121 fan.*

Winch hooks hanging over
the Q121 testing platform.

The author standing in front of the third set of turning blades within the return tunnel.

The exterior of the Grade 1 listed Q121 building.

The author standing in front of the 30'-diameter fan duct for scale purposes. The large mahogany fan blades could create a wind speed of around 130 mph to test the entire airframe of early aircraft.

Exterior signage.

Looking past the Q121 fan to the first set of turning blades from the working section/testing platform. The fan sucked air into the tunnel.

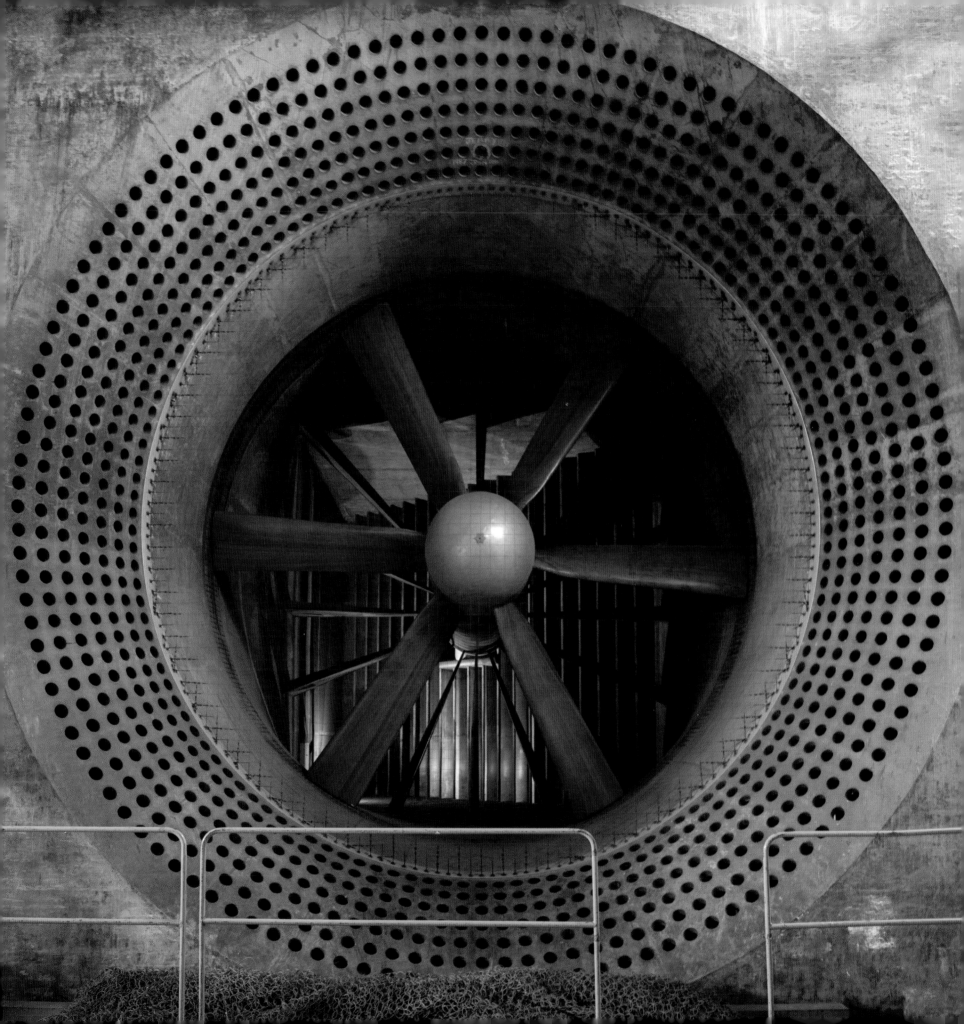

The main return tunnel inside the wooden seven-foot tunnel in the R52 building.

Amp meters in the R52 building.

The tunnel controllers desk for the seven foot transonic tunnel. R52 Building.

The contraction in tunnel diameter between the settling chamber and the working section is what creates the high wind velocity required to test items at transonic speeds (around the sound barrier).

Control panel at the wind tunnel controllers desk. R52 building.

Surviving Motor from 1916, Electrical Construction Company Ltd.

Controllers desk in the R52 building.

Entrance to the R52 building.

Abandoned Farmhouse
Luxembourg

We visited this peculiar mishmash of a building in a lush rural valley on a trip through Belgium, Luxembourg and France at the end of 2013. Having the precise coordinates for a location loaded into your sat-nav is no guarantee that the building will simply present itself to you on arrival. The announcement "You have reached your destination" simply brought us up alongside a busy Bavarian-style bar, crammed with locals drinking large glasses of frothy beer. A few at the window eyed our GB-plated vehicle with a degree of suspicion. Or maybe I just felt a sense of guilt; being in foreign lands about to attempt access to a private building can have that effect.

We drove off looking for signs of an abandoned structure, eventually spotting something surrounded by trees along a track leading away from the busy bar. If we walked down this track we would risk being spotted, so we parked out of sight of the bar and took a direct route across fields to reach the cluster of trees. The trees did indeed shelter the building we were looking for, although not using the track meant we had to trek through thick brambles and nettle beds to reach it. Scratched and stung we arrived in front of the structure, but at least no one knew we were there!

The exterior of the remote farmhouse and mill.

The building had clearly been built over quite a period of time and had been extended several times to incorporate various working functions. To our left was once a mill. A hidden stream ran along the side and inside there were remnants of grinding machinery. The central part, which looked to have been added later, encompassed all the living areas. And the right side opened into a large barn with hayloft.

The front door was conveniently left ajar; a gentle push and we were inside. It was gloomy and tight. Furniture and other items were left in places that made it look as though the owners had just popped out to the shops. Drawers opened to trinkets and handwritten letters, while wardrobes revealed thick fur coats and smart jackets. The beds were made and a supply of various medicines was packed inside a small wooden chest in the bathroom. Derelict or abandoned residential locations are always so much more interesting when filled with these human touches; they help to tell the story of those who lived there and maybe hold clues as to why they no longer do.

For me the most interesting room was the kitchen: a glorious old range cooker sat at one end next to a small wooden work surface and a stool, chopped wood sat in a basket nearby, shelves were packed with pots and pans, an old crucifix hung above the kitchen table, paint was peeling from the walls all around.

The light from the kitchen window cast a diffused autumn glow across the interior; the arrangement of rustic elements within made it feel as though I were standing in a painting by Vermeer. I set the tripod and camera up to shoot the cooker end of the room and captured the scene across a series of bracketed exposures. The images that flashed up on the camera's screen indeed looked like I was on assignment for the Delft School of Photography. To this day the shot of the cooker is one of my favourite images.

Lastly, I moved into the barn. The space below the hayloft was low and cobwebs hung so thickly that they brushed my head. However, I didn't actually see any spiders in there!

Since our visit the property has been entirely cleared of belongings. Hopefully that means it is about to undergo some kind of redevelopment and journey back to habitation.

Anyway, I'll leave it there and let the images tell the rest of the story.

One of the windows in the cobweb-filled barn.

*The scene found
in the dining room
of the farmhouse.
No doubt other
photographers had
set up the still life
on the table.*

Colin's Barn

Cotswolds, UK

There are some buildings that don't fit into any of the normal architectural categories, their unique strangeness defying classification. Although this stone construction started life simply as an unusual hay barn, it evolved over time into a sprawling expression of one man's creativity.

After an accident in the late 1980s, a local man was awarded compensation and decided to buy himself some land to begin sheep farming. As Colin moved around his new land he found his fields littered with shards of Cotswold stone, so he began work on a dry stone wall project. In his own words, "It was only supposed to be a barn to keep hay dry but I kind of got carried away". Over the next eleven years the barn grew outwards to form walls, sheep pens, dovecotes, turrets, rooms and a raised loft area where he would sometimes sleep during lambing season.

The enigmatic exterior of Colin's Barn.

In the late 90s, a sizeable quantity of marble was found nearby and a quarrying company moved in to begin extraction. The noise created by the quarrying activities forced Colin to sell up and move. It was abandoned in 2000 and nature has gradually been reclaiming the site ever since.

I first visited the barn back in the summer 2014 with Rebecca Bathory, another heritage photographer whose work I greatly admire. We had just spent a few hours exploring the labyrinth of tunnels within Box Quarry below the nearby town of Corsham and decided to make the short detour to see Colin's Barn on our way home.

We had heard that the quarry company was not fond of visitors as the only access to the barn was along the same track that their lorries used. We made our way swiftly along the track and over the gate into the field without being spotted. The barn was unlike anything we had seen before, like a dry stone wall on steroids.

Many visitors and photographers have dubbed it 'The Hobbit House'. Despite it not being sunk into the side of a hill or having a large round wooden front door, it certainly felt like something from Tolkein's Middle Earth. I have read that Colin is not fond of his creation being referred to as a Hobbit House, but these things have a habit of being linked with popular culture and so the name has stuck.

We began shooting the exterior from a limited number of angles, hampered by the thick undergrowth crowding the structure. Inside, the rooms were bare and gloomy and not particularly inspiring photographically. It's a small location but one that provided some strong images.

After about an hour we heard the unmistakable sound of a heavy vehicle on the track next to us. The vehicle stopped, the engine cut out and a cab door was slammed; leaving our own vehicle parked on the grass verge a short distance from the entrance maybe hadn't been the best idea. I hid behind a dovecote while Rebecca lay down with her gear in the long grass. I watched as the driver approached Rebecca's position, stopped then glared down into the long grass in front of him. Rebecca peered up at him and received a loud shouting at from point blank range. I appeared and received the same – it was time for us to leave.

I visited the location a second time shortly after having my old camera converted to IR, enabling it to capture wavelengths within the Infrared spectrum. Each summer the location is engulfed by foliage, making it the perfect subject for IR photography. (Chlorophyll within plant's leaves reflects the Infrared wavelengths in sunlight making them turn white, producing a very otherworldly effect in the final image.) Fortunately, I managed to stay undetected on this second visit as I turned up at dawn on a Sunday.

Sooner rather than later this location will inevitably succumb to the plant life that invades it a little more each year. When it does, the UK will have lost a truly unique folly.

Another view of the barn, showing one of the outer-lying walls with dovecotes.

Following page: A five shot Infrared panorama showing most of the extensive structure.

Abandoned Educational Institute

Belgium

I usually try to find out some background info for a location before photographing it; it tends to make the experience of being there more rewarding when you know what you are looking at. Sometimes the information is plentiful and easy to find, while at other times there seems to be nothing available. On our arrival at this abandoned education faculty in the middle of a busy Belgian city centre we had no idea of its real name, when it opened or closed or what was taught there. Only through researching the location for this book did I eventually manage to discover some interesting historical facts about this impressive building.

The campus was founded by Georges Montefiore-Levi, a metallurgical engineer, who had made a substantial amount of money by securing a patent for phosphor bronze. Due to its conductivity and resistance to heat, this alloy of copper could be used within electrical components; it could be cast to create rust-resistant items such as bearings and boat propellers; and most importantly, it could be used in telephone cables. Phosphor bronze played a major role in the creation of the Belgian telephone network.

The grand exterior of the Montefiore Electrical Institute.

After attending the First International Exhibition of Electrical Engineering in Paris in 1881, Montefiore became very aware of the potential in this emerging field of knowledge. He decided to set up a school of excellence to provide Belgian society with the skilled electrical engineers it would need in the years to come. After approaching the state with his proposal, he was offered the site of the abandoned 'Ecole Centrale'. Within two years the site had been cleared up and the classrooms filled with equipment bought using Georges' own money. The 'Montefiore Electrical Institute' was opened in October 1883.

By the late 1880s the number of students applying to the Institute had grown to such an extent that larger premises were needed, so the site was transferred to the nearby campus we visited. The school continued to grow and by 1903, Montefiore had financed the construction of a huge on-site amphitheatre that would seat over 300 students. Its design and layout was heavily influenced by Faraday's famous lecture hall at the Royal Institution in London.

The site continued to train engineers in various fields – including electrical, mechanical and radio engineering – until 1977, when it was decided that the Institute had outgrown the campus and it was moved to one of the larger universities in the city. Back in 2010 plans were discussed to regenerate the site. As yet, nothing has happened.

The now derelict Institute is located in a busy part of the city, which makes gaining entry to the locked up campus a tricky endeavour. A double set of metal gates bars the way into the open area in front of the main buildings; negotiating them in full view of the many people passing by was fairly nerve-racking. Once beyond the gates, the impressive main frontage of the Institute can be enjoyed.

The main building features a central block with two perpendicular side wings. The classically inspired exterior has many beautiful features, such as a semicircular pediment featuring a crest with the moto *L'Union Fait la Force* (Unity Makes Strength), and on the forward-facing ends of the side wings, six carved high-relief stone tablets showing political and cultural motifs.

The rooms and corridors inside the building are mostly bare, with much of the equipment and furniture having been relocated to the new university campus. In a few places there are signs of the teaching that took place; a jumble of desks in an upper floor classroom; a cupboard full of textbooks and paperwork.

Across the courtyard an open door leads into the building housing the large auditorium. Inside, the rooms are again mostly bare, but two of them feature something quite majestic. The lecture theatre is a sight to behold, its rows of seating still intact and spread across two floors. A moment lingering in the silence here leads one to wonder what it was like when a lecture was in full swing, the seats packed with over 300 students. Just a few rooms away is an absolutely stunning architectural staircase, bathed in a soft pool of light below a skylight. Prior to arriving, I had no idea that the stairs were here so walking into this room was a real 'wow' moment.

There were parts of the campus that we could not access on the day, such as a stunning wood-panelled room with a grand table and impressive chandelier. A good reason to return the next time I find myself in the area.

A grand staircase just outside the three-hundred-seat auditorium.

Desks in a top floor classroom.

*Close-up of
the grand staircase.*

Ground floor corridor.

The large lecture auditorium that was built in 1903.

Ruined Gwrych Castle
Abergele, North Wales, UK

Driving along the A55, the North Wales coastal road that skirts the Irish Sea, you will pass a junction for a town called Abergele. Inland and set back from the town, nestled against a wooded hillside, is an impressive stretch of ramparts and towers. This imposing structure is the magnificent Gwrych Castle and has stood here for nearly two hundred years.

The view along the entire castle from Hesketh Tower.

Although it's called Gwrych Castle, the structure is actually a large country house built to resemble a castle. It was built for Lloyd Hesketh Bamford Hesketh in 1819, a property owner with estates in North Wales, North West England and Lancashire. The house was then passed down to his son Robert, who in turn bequeathed it onto his daughter, Winifred, Countess of Dundonald. The castle remained within the care of the Dundonald family until the Second World War, when it was used by the Britsh government to house Jewish children, refugees from the horrors happening across the channel. After the war, the castle changed ownership several times and for a short spell was open to the public with medieval re-enactments taking place in the grounds. It was also used as a training venue for boxing champion Randolph Turpin.

Since 1985, the castle has not been maintained and has deteriorated rapidly. The legendary wet climate in Wales, together with looting and vandalism, have taken their toll on the structure and today all that remains of this site that was once called 'The Showpiece of Wales' is a derelict shell covered in bushes and trees.

During the 1990s, 12-year-old Mark Baker began campaigning to have the castle restored to its former glory. Baker played an instrumental role in the formation of the Gwrych Castle Preservation Trust which today, with its army of enthusiastic volunteers, looks after the castle and its grounds. Ownership currently resides with a hotel consortium that plans to convert the castle into a 75-bedroom luxury hotel.

On the day we visited all was quiet at the site. We parked up some distance away and made our way along a farmer's track that led to the castle grounds. Again we went a little too far with our stealth approach! As we discovered once we arrived, the public are allowed to walk right up to the castle but not beyond the palisade fencing that secures the site. Gaps could be found all around the perimeter and access proved easy enough. Like some ancient jungle-bound fortress, exploring her feels like you are re-discovering something that has been lost for centuries.

A maze of rubble-strewn basement rooms with high walls stretches up for several floors. An occasional stone staircase rises to isolated sections of first floor rooms, although they don't extend far before collapse is met. Any floors above the first have given way many years previously, leaving peculiar fireplaces and other features stranded way up high where there was once a room.

Passing through the middle of the castle from east to west is a small track. It winds its way through arches and gently downhill past the stone walls to a large gatehouse. At several points along the route, gaps in the security fencing allow access to paths on the wooded hillside behind the castle. From these paths you can find your way to the tallest towers that dominate the vista from the coastal road. They provide a series of stunning views across the whole complex. The central tower overlooks what was the main living area of the castle, although trees now grow up and out of the rooms below. At the far western end of the complex, 'Hesketh Tower' (the tallest) provides an impressive view along the entire structure, stretching eastwards for over 300m.

The story of this location may yet have a happy ending: work continues enthusiastically at the site as volunteers clear undergrowth, revealing more of the structure from beneath dense foliage. All that remains now is for the hotel group to make good its plans to restore the site. Despite places like this looking fantastic in an abandoned state, it's always nice to hear that they may be given a second chance. If and when the time comes that Gwrych Castle is a 5-star hotel, I shall return and reshoot the images again for comparison.

A view of what was the main living quarters from another of the castle's towers. The town of Abergele can be seen in the background.

One of the archways
that spans the track
that winds its way east
to west through
the entire complex.

At the time these pictures were taken, the castle was covered in dense undergrowth. Efforts have been made since to clear the foliage from the structure and turn the castle back into an attraction for the area.

One of the windows in the main living quarters. The rest of the structure is just a façade.

The castle is set against a beautiful wooded backdrop with views looking north to the Irish Sea.

Subterranean Reservoirs and Cisterns

Various Locations

Having shot inside a wide variety of structures, it's a real pleasure to photograph something that is a radical break from the norm. I have always been fascinated by subterranean locations; prior to shooting abandoned heritage I was involved in the South Wales caving community and would spend weekends exploring the labyrinthine passageways far below the Llangattock hills near Abergavenny. There is something quite visceral, thrilling and secretive about exploring deep below the everyday plane of human existence, the people above oblivious to the hidden world below their feet. It is logical that such a world exists in the porous and rain-soaked limestone hills of South Wales, but the discovery that an equally vast network of hidden and varied underground spaces exists below urban centres can be quite surprising.

London is well known to have one of the UK's largest underground networks, from sewers and culverts, tube and service tunnels, cable runs and infrastructure, bunkers and cellars to the more secretive government- and intelligence-owned areas. This hidden city calls to the curious and adventurous among us, who, once the sun has set, slip silently across the public/private divide into ladder-lined shafts and tunnel entrances, clicking on head torches before vanishing into the darkness. For me, much of what can be explored beneath cities carries an increased risk of prosecution. For this reason, I have restricted my trips to isolated and disused areas.

The view along one of several brick lanes inside a large Victorian era cistern.

The first of these trips came in late 2013. We parked alongside one of London's large open spaces, grabbed our gear and headed off across the grass. Arriving at the co-ordinates, we found the manhole cover set into a concrete cap, surrounded by a perimeter of Heras fencing. A park pavilion silhouetted against the light-polluted sky of the city rang out with voices, most likely just drunks or teenagers hanging out, but it always makes entry feel riskier when people may be watching.

Once past the fence we got out the drain keys, slotted them into the manhole cover and twisted, lifting the very heavy cover up and off. An open brick-lined shaft with rungs set into the sides led down into the unknown. These moments are a fabulous mix of foreboding and adrenaline.

I stepped onto the iron ladder and started downwards, only clicking on my head torch once it was hidden below the top of the shaft. To my surprise the bottom of the ladder was just below my feet. On my left a set of steps headed downwards again; we set off and emerged at the corner of what seemed to be a vast subterranean space formed by repeating rows of beautifully crafted brick arches. Each row was separated by a low wall and in the bottom of each row a small amount of residual water remained. The space was about 80 metres wide with each row around 120 metres long. Its size, symmetry, repetition and the exacting perfection of its Victorian craftsman builders stunned us; that something designed to be filled with water and invisible to the public should be made to be so beautiful says a lot about the values held dear during those times. It also says a lot about the principles guiding modern builds with regards to cost over craftsmanship. This structure was completed in 1868 and it's still solid, built to last. I wondered how many Londoners walked overhead every day and knew nothing of the existence of this magnificent space?

Cisterns, designed for the collection and storage of water, feature watertight linings in their construction. They are generally enclosed under a roof or underground to prevent sunlight causing the growth of algae. And they are often found in areas where water is scarce or needed for agricultural irrigation. Due to health concerns, modern-day cisterns are rarely used to store drinking water.

My companion that night was one of the UK's most talented light artists. We were separated from each other within the cistern by about five of the brick rows so as not to not pollute each other's shots with unwanted light. That's the beauty of photographing a space such as this – there is no natural light at all, so you must bring your own with you to help create the image. You choose where to add the light, the shape, colour and duration. In short, light painting is one of the more creative pursuits in photography.

I set my tripod and camera up looking symmetrically along the centre of a row and set it to bulb mode (bulb mode holds the camera shutter open for as long as bulb mode is activated). This leaves you free to walk around the scene 'painting in' the light. The camera shutter may be open but the scene in front of it is dark and no image is recorded on the camera sensor. I wanted the entire length of brick arches down to the far end to be illuminated evenly in the final shot and so I moved into the right-side neighbouring row. For this shot the key thing was not to give the camera a direct view of the light source, which would create an unwanted bright starburst effect.

Sunlight punches through the gloom within a covered reservoir. Part of a water treatment works.

Getting into position, hidden out of sight behind the first brick column, I turned my Scurion lamp on to its flood setting, facing it sideways to light up the opposite side of the row. After six seconds I hid the lamp by pressing it into my chest, moving forwards into the next arch where I repeated the process for a further six seconds. I did this in every arch until I ran out of cistern. Turning off the lamp I then moved across the row in which the camera was set up, trying not to fall into the water in the total darkness. Once in the left-side neighbouring row I repeated the process, lighting up the as-yet-unlit side all the way back to the camera, again using six seconds in each arch. The shot took about 15 minutes to light but the end result was well worth the effort. It did make me wonder if the original construction crew and architect had ever seen it lit up like this – multiple lights would be needed but using this technique required just a single light source and some time.

I did a further three trips into this subterranean wonderland, capturing it from different angles and using different light positions. Each of the trips thrilled me just as much as the previous ones. But all good things come to an end. The company that owned it realised people had been getting in and eventually put a proper cover on it.

Shortly after my final trip, an online contact told me of a second covered reservoir located somewhere below the capital. He kindly agreed to meet me after dark and guide me to the location.

Arriving after nightfall we encountered a low domed hill surrounded by a small fence and a line of trees. We made our way up to the crest of the hill and lifted the hatch. Although not as big as the previous location, this one was circular in layout with support pillars radiating outwards from a central brick core that housed the access ladder from the surface. The feel was very different but still very visually impressive.

The curved outer edge of the structure provided almost perfect acoustics, an echo to rival the one of St Paul's Whispering Gallery. Again the craftsmanship and quality of the brickwork was of an incredibly high standard and it was still in exceptional condition 170 years after its construction. We spent an enjoyable evening taking several photographs of its interior but have not managed to make it back since.

The following year we were on a trip shooting several locations in Lincolnshire. On the way home we had the chance to visit our third subterranean reservoir – this time a small hexagonal water tank located below a landscaped garden that formed part of a historic waterworks in Leicestershire. A central raised grassy platform with a stone gazebo and steps formed the roof of the underground space, with the gazebo providing an air inlet. Around the raised area were six ponds that acted as filter beds draining into the main tank.

It wasn't quite so obvious how to gain access and we spent a good ten minutes looking for a way in. Eventually we found the cover and we were soon inside. This one had a totally different feel to the previous two; sunk just below ground-level and built using a much darker brick, it included six small ground level windows that allowed bright shafts of light to penetrate the gloom.

There was some restoration work being carried out in one half of the tank so the space available for photography was limited. After ten minutes gathering up several hundred tealight candles that had been left there from a previous shoot we got to work. The shafts of light were a real treat and we found ourselves waiting for the next break in the clouds before rattling off a series of shots until the beams dimmed and vanished.

Shooting underground adds something extra to an already exciting and fascinating hobby. I am looking forward to shooting more of these amazing spaces, perhaps some of the ancient cisterns located beneath cities such as El Jadida in Morocco or the world famous Basilica Cistern beneath Istanbul.

The central brick core of the circular cistern. The access ladder was housed within.

Looking along the length
of one of the brick rows in
the largest cistern I visited.

Abandoned Toolmakers Factory
Northern England

This location is somewhere I had wanted to photograph for a long time and has to be one of the more atmospheric and fascinating places we have visited. Situated in a busy industrial town in northern England, this old tool factory dates back to 1836, when it first opened at another nearby location. By 1852 the business had grown enough to require new premises, so it relocated to its current location.

The factory was a leading specialist manufacturer of shears, files, mallets, knives, edgers and punches for leather workers and the shoemaking industry.

Over the years, technical advances in the factories that produced the vast majority of our shoes had pushed craftsman shoemakers out of business along with the businesses that provided them with the tools of their trade. This particular factory closed its doors in 2004.

Work benches and storage areas at the front of this historic factory.

Our visit was an impromptu one; a new photographer acquaintance and I decided we would drive up to the two planned locations after work on a Friday night, stay in a local hotel and set our alarm clocks for an early start.

After a poor night's sleep we were quickly up and out into the still sleeping streets of this rain-soaked town. We arrived at the gates to the courtyard that gave access to the rear of the factory only to find them locked. Perplexed, we scanned the block for an alternative way in but decided instead to head off to the second location (the town's abandoned law courts) and return later in the day to see if the situation had changed.

At the law courts we met another photographer I knew who updated us on another way in to the factory. By midday we were back and soon climbing over the final wall that dropped us into the adjoining yard behind the factory.

Several empty brick sheds were the first structures we encountered. One contained hanging chains and winch gear; in another were the remains of the company's power generation, flywheels and belts, mostly suspended from the roof – the engines that powered them were long gone.

Moving on through a narrow alley, we passed between the broken remains of the workshops and storage areas: buddleia bushes and nettles sprouting from gaps in the shattered concrete underfoot; ivy working its way into door frames; broken glass in the windows and a stillness presiding over it all. Standing within this scene, we too were stunned into silence. Despite the location having travelled far along its road to collapse, there was still a tangible presence here; you got a real sense the past and of the building's purpose and history.

Moving inside and up a flight of worn wooden steps, we emerged into a large room with wooden floors, workbenches in the centre of the room and cupboards around the outer walls. There were tools left lying about and wood shavings scattered across work surfaces. It was obvious that the staff had simply stopped work one day, gone home and never returned. In other rooms were rows of box cupboards that filled entire walls, some doors labelled in chalk, indicating the types of materials that would have been found inside.

Each new room we entered was like a museum of old industry, frozen in time since the day the place closed. On one of the upper floors we found a small office in the corner of one of the workshops, just big enough for someone to sit at the writing desk. It felt like something straight out of a Dickens novel.

Parts of the site have started to collapse and the buildings are likely to be demolished if the decay continues. Between two of the buildings we found an enclosed wooden bridge linking the first floors together. Any attempt to cross the 3 metre span of rotten timber would have resulted in both you and it crashing to the ground below. When you see this level of decay in a location it acts as a red flag; you slow right down, tread much more carefully, testing spongy floors with the speculative nudge of an extended foot while stood within a doorframe. In gloomy interiors such as these, staying safe can be a tricky business.

After around three hours inside the location, our bad night's sleep was beginning to catch up with us. We had a few hours in the car ahead of us so we called it a day. It's a fascinating location and one that I would like to revisit at some point . . . if it's still standing!

An alleyway between the workshops and storage areas. The wooden bridge between them is on the verge of collapse.

A tiny supervisor's office on the upper floor of the factory. Through the windows, it overlooked a large area of work benches.

A stair climbs from
the factory to
the attic area where
raw materials used
in the manufacturing
process were stored.

Country Estate Ruins
North Wales, UK

While travelling in Cambodia in 1997, I made the first of two trips to the jungle-bound ruins of the ancient city of Angkor Thom and its many palaces and temples, including its most famous temple, Angkor Wat. Many of the structures that make up this vast historical site have been restored and it is well known as one of the crown jewels of Unesco World Heritage, ranking alongside the Pyramids at Giza and Machu Pichu in Peru.

In 1860 the French explorer Henri Mouhot reached Angkor. Although the structures within the city were largely hidden by thick jungle undergrowth, they were clearly the remains of the mighty Khmer civilisation. The moment when this lost city was revealed to Mouhot must have been thrilling. I remember wondering at the time if there could be other places in the world where such mighty structures remained undiscovered; maybe somewhere in the Amazon Basin or the jungles of sub-Sahara Africa. I certainly wouldn't have expected to find something reminiscent of these ancient ruins back home in the United Kingdom! Yet in North Wales, hidden among thick woodland, is an expansive set of structures that once formed an important country estate.

Stone steps in what were the gardens at the rear of the main house, now almost invisible under the ferns and weeds that have taken hold.

Much of the large house at the centre of the estate has been a roofless ruin since the Second World War. The original house was constructed on the hillside here in 1618, with later remodelling work carried out in 1776. Built for the dominant family and landowners of the area, it has hosted royalty, played a small role in the English civil war and been a barracks for soldiers. Rumour has it that during the outbreak of the Second World War, Polish soldiers were billeted at the property. It was winter and the interior was bitterly cold. After complaining and failing to get stationed in warmer quarters, the soldiers started a small fire in an effort to persuade the British army the house was not suitable. The fire quickly got out of hand and a large part of it burned down. As a result, all the soldiers achieved was to be moved into even colder cabins in the estate grounds.

Since then the estate has been left in the care of nature. In the almost 80 years that have passed, the gardens have grown across everything, rain has finished the work the fire started and time has rendered the follies and outbuildings unwitting participants in a wonderful game of hide and seek. There are so many structures littered around the grounds that finding them all requires some ingenuity and effort on the part of the visitor. On the outskirts of the estate the gatehouse can be found by a stone bridge; its wrought iron gates, visible in old photographs, are now nowhere to be seen. Following this same route a wonderfully atmospheric folly is encountered. A curved colonnade built into a vertically cut embankment marks the transition between what had been the upper and lower lawns. Inside the colonnade is a stone stairway; descend and you will emerge from between pillars into an area of greenhouses where vegetables for the house were grown. Being unable to see for more than several metres due to the thick profusion of laurel bushes and ferns means you just happen across garden features and structures.

Eventually you encounter the looming bulk of the main house, trees and bushes growing right up against the walls and even inside the rooms. Despite being less than half as old as Angkor it has a similar feel to it; exploring it is like re-discovering something lost in time. Moving around the exterior you discover scenes where nature has made features out of the mundane; drainpipes act as conduits for creeping ivy, pillars and stonework crumble under the relentless bombardment of changes in season and all that was once new begins to break down as it is recycled. Given time, nature conquers and destroys everything in her path.

Within the walls of the house, the rooms at ground level are a jumble of rotting timber and foliage. The lack of any first and second floors means that fireplaces and ovens are stranded high up on the walls. The scene of devastation is quite surreal. Moving from room to room through internal portals that once were doors, it's hard to imagine the splendour that previously filled this void. Indeed it is a sobering thought that the buildings we know and love could one day end up in a similar state. The privileged occupants who lived out their days here never imagined that their grand home and immaculate gardens would end up a lonely but beautiful ruin in the woods.

Ruined portico at the front entrance to the house.

The skeletal remains of greenhouses within the grounds. The glass, unseen, crunches underfoot, hidden by ferns.

*Doorways and
a corridor inside
what was once one
of several outbuildings
in the estate.*

*Close up on
the main stairs within
the ruins of the house.*

*Ferns grow
from the floor of
an interior room
at a lodge within
the grounds.*

A doorway that
once led out into
the back lawns,
now a forest.

The ruins of a colonnade in the grounds. A staircase can be found inside that transitioned from what was the upper to the lower lawns.

Satellite Communication Station
Belgium (Demolished)

One of the first locations on our European trip in February 2014 brought us to the small village of Kester, located in rolling countryside just outside of Brussels. We were here to experience a first for our little photography group – the interior of an abandoned ex-military radome, one of those 'golf ball-like' geodesic structures beyond the fence lines of communication bases.

Inside the large radome.

Construction of this NATO installation, codenamed 'Zone Braams', began in 1969. It was operational by 1971 and manned by a small contingent of mostly US military personnel up until its closure in late 2012. It was one of several stations dotted around Europe designed to maintain secure military communications between NATO member states.

Within a high perimeter fence there were two structures; the large dome mounted atop the westernmost of these. The buildings were at one stage filled with electronic monitoring equipment but had been completely stripped out save for the large antenna within the dome. The dome is constructed using a rigid geodesic frame covered in a fabric made from PTFE, a 'Teflon-like' material that does not interfere with the antenna signals while protecting it from the weather and keeping it hidden from view.

We had heard that the entire site was on the verge of demolition, with diggers actually moving in just three months later. There are plans to build a new modern NATO Satcom installation on the same site, which will feature 4 inflatable domes of a slightly smaller size.

Entry was very easy through a hole in the outer fence. And the doors into the buildings were left unlocked. Once inside we climbed some stairs and emerged onto the main floor of the dome. It was a strange experience being within a sphere containing a large satellite dish. Light filtered in through the PTFE fabric, casting a strange, warm glow over everything.

Photographing was tricky due to the close proximity of the antenna and the wide angle of view required to get it all in shot. So I opted to shoot panoramic images. While inside, the setting sun increased the warmth of the light even more, filling the dome with deep orange tones. It was an interesting and visually striking place to photograph and we headed to our hotel more than satisfied with the shots we had taken.

As the sun set outside the orange glow of the transmitted light within intensified.

The exterior
of the radome
after the sun
had set.

Within the dish of the antenna.

Abandoned Textile Mill
South West England

Textile production in England is an ancient craft that dates back to Tudor times. Prior to the Industrial Revolution, textiles were produced on a relatively small scale by artisan weavers, usually working within their own homes, often for a master or craft guild. As time progressed and textile making technologies improved, factories were set up with machinery that accelerated production quotas and brought the different stages of production under one roof. The many valleys in the landscape of rolling hills contained fast-flowing streams, which proved very useful to factories employing water power to run the machines. The area was also popular with sheep farmers and this provided a local supply of the raw fleece required to produce a variety of woollen end products.

Carts used for transporting the cloth around the factory lie dormant in a corner of the main factory.

In 1754 Edward Fox married into the Were family and together they set up a textile factory producing woollen products on the banks of a local river. The company was set up just as the Industrial Revolution took hold and over the next 20 years the company's assets multiplied. During this time, Thomas Fox (brother to Edward) also became a partner in the business; he had recently returned from Germany and the Netherlands where he had gained valuable knowledge of the techniques used in European textile production. These skills were incorporated into the new company and gave the company an edge in the market place.

During the 1790s, the company purchased an old flour mill and warehouse complex a short distance away and moved most of the production into these larger premises. The older site was retained as a dyeing and finishing factory for the completed cloth. At its height during the 1800s, the new site employed more than 3500 people from the immediate area and was the largest woollen mill in the South West, able to produce 6400 metres of cloth per day. As well as being one of the biggest mills in the UK, the site has the added distinction of being one of the first makers of flannel. It also developed the khaki dye used for military uniforms during the Second Boer War. During the First World War an order from the War Office requested they produce nearly 1400 kilometres of khaki cloth for soldiers' puttees. The company was very busy and very profitable.

The factory continued to produce cloth until the 1990s when dwindling demand for such a large site forced it to close down. The modern-day company, still within the same village, occupies a more compact site with a much smaller workforce, but it is still producing high quality award-winning textiles.

Our visit came in the summer of 2014. We visited the older part of the site first and once inside we were struck with just what an incredible time capsule the place is. A lot of the machinery is still in-situ; rows of vats, jigs and frames designed to wash the fleece, tease the nap or dye the cloth sit in neat lines. Hanging down from above are a series of cogs, wheels and belts – part of a power system that connected to a water wheel in the centre of the factory. Carts that were used to transport the cloth are left littered around. The location could be a 'museum of textile production during the Industrial Revolution, but in making it safe for visitors it would sadly lose something of its authenticity. It's one of the reasons visiting such an incredible site in a small group is such a privilege, like being part of an archaeological dig uncovering a small part of our history. I appreciate that the real work on this front has already been done by historians and heritage experts, but from the point of view of a photographer this experience feels authentic and exciting. And besides, taking the photographs and sharing them online is still reaching a whole new audience.

Machinery in the dye house, the wheels that ran the machines via a series of belts can be seen above.

There is only a small remaining part of the heavily rusted water wheel, but to see the methods they devised to drive the machinery in an age before electricity was something to behold. Just outside the factory walls, Thomas Fox had ordered the digging of two large basins to collect water from the River Tone. The factory could now control the flow of water precisely, running it when it was needed and conserving it when it was not required. The factory features several stone channels set into the floor where the water flowed in from the basins to drive the wheel. After turning the wheel, the water dropped into a tunnel beneath the factory and out into a natural stream.

A fascinating bit of machinery was discovered in one corner of the factory, the name of which I have since discovered to be a teasel napper. It features a rotating barrel with thistle (teasel) seed heads clamped onto its surface. As the barrel rotated, the teasel heads plucked and raised fibres from the surface of the cloth. This was known as raising the nap and left a soft, fuzzy, uneven surface on one side. An experienced worker would then shear the fibres close to the cloth, leaving a soft, velvety finish.

After a couple of hours within the oldest part of the site we moved the short distance along the road to the much larger buildings that were occupied during the 1790s. This location features a huge array of structures, but after spending too long in the dye house we were running out of time, so we only managed to see a small part of it. First was a large empty warehouse area with a huge piece of street art on one of the walls. I hate seeing anything sprayed onto walls in heritage buildings and could never condone it, however this 3 metre tall stencilled alien was very impressive and must have taken the artist a long time to produce.

With time quickly running out, we shot into the main factory building and made our way to the top floor where we found the Autoconer machines. The symmetrical photo between these two winding machines is one of the classic shots from this location; we shot it from a couple of angles and we were done. There is so much more to photograph at this site; provided it is still accessible we will return another time.

A teasel napper machine, designed to raise the nap on the surface of the woolen cloth.

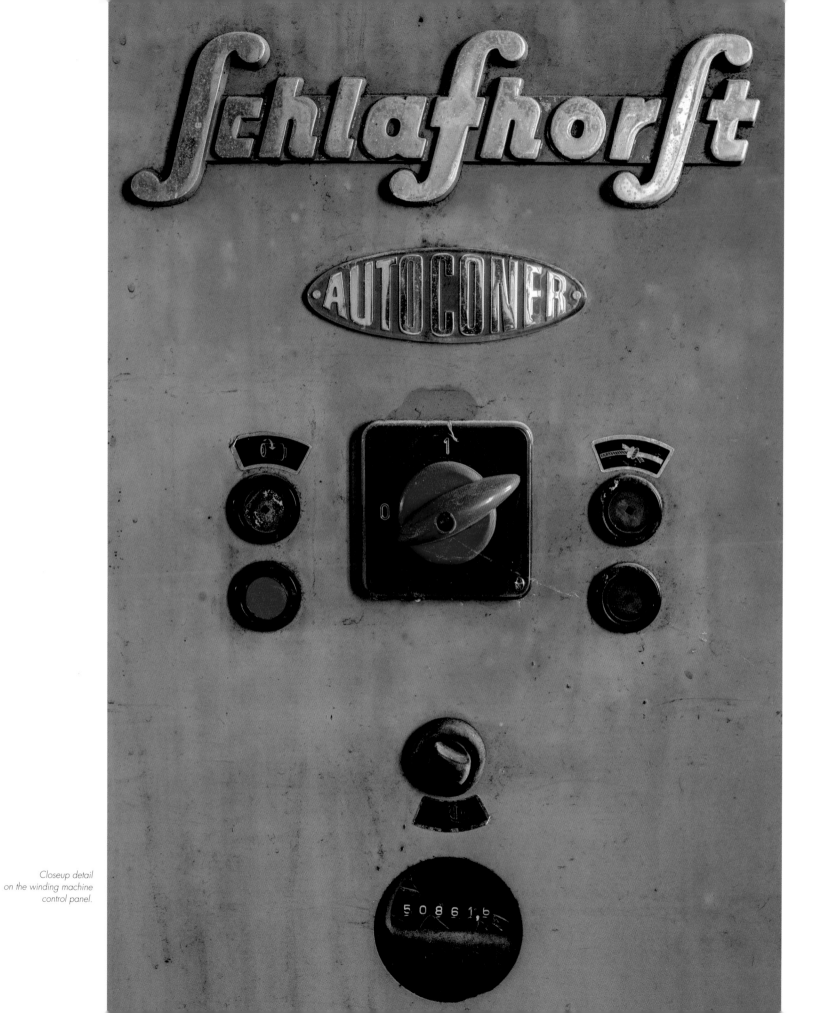

Closeup detail on the winding machine control panel.

Auto-coner winding machines located in the newer part of site.

Looking down
behind the numerous
washing vats on
the main factory floor.

A chain guard and
cogged wheels on
the side of a machine
in the main factory.

The remains of the large water wheel that powered the oldest part of the site.

Weeds grow from gaps in the floor in the area of several dye vats.

A nine foot high
bit of art sprayed onto
the walls in one of
the empty warehouse
buildings on site.

Machine rollers
and parts stacked up
on a cart.

Cloth draped down
a wall in the dye house.

Machinery from
the Industrial
Revolution on
the main
factory floor.

Royal Hospital Haslar

Gosport, UK

Late in 2015, a researcher for a production company contacted me to discuss an idea for shooting a three-part pilot of short films on the United Kingdoms's abandoned heritage. I had been approached by two other companies in the preceding months with similar ideas but had declined based upon how they wished to present the content. The difference this time would be that permission to film would be obtained and the focus would be on each location and its history. After agreeing to work with the company, I was tasked with securing three different and interesting locations. This made a refreshing change to shooting a location, having the owner on board and with their offer of a fee waiver greatly appreciated. We had Eric from the Haslar Heritage Group turn up on the day and show us around whilst giving a fascinating talk on the history of the building.

A spiral staircase that connects all of the floors in the front wing of the hospital.

Arriving at the front gate security office earlier than planned, we were waved through, shown where to park and invited in for coffee while we waited for the rest of the crew to turn up. The conversation came around to warning us of a likely encounter we would have while on site.

"They call themselves urbex," he said. "They travel down here from all over the country and try and get inside the buildings with their cameras, so it's my job to catch them and chuck them out. I don't understand it all, personally." He had many amusing stories to tell about his never-ending battle of wills with the site's almost daily 'unofficial visitors'.

Access to the second location of the three had been arranged for the Royal Hospital Haslar in Gosport on the UK's south coast. It's one of the oldest abandoned locations I have photographed and has an important history going back over 260 years. Designed by Theodore Jacobsen, an amateur architect, the hospital was constructed between 1746 and 1761 and partially opened as a dedicated Naval Hospital in 1753.

Built right on the quayside, it included its own dock close to the main building where ships could unload patients and sailors injured during battle. Between October 29 and November 3, 1805, shortly after the historic and spectacular victory at the Battle of Trafalgar, some 134 injured were unloaded from ships such as the world famous HMS Victory and the Fighting Temeraire. A tramway led from the quayside, through the main gate, across the yard and into the hospital's arcade, where patients were transferred to stretchers and moved to the treatment areas. In addition to those from the Napoleonic Wars, the hospital has also seen patients admitted from conflicts such as the Crimean and Boer Wars, as well as the First and Second World Wars.

A prominent researcher and doctor, Jame Lind, began working at Haslar in 1758. He had previously carried out the first ever clinical trial in medical history by the use of citrus fruits to counter scurvy on Naval ships (1747). An early pioneer into the study of tropical diseases, he published an important paper on Typhus in 1763.

With The Royal Haslar claiming the illustrious title as the longest serving dedicated military hospital, it finally closed its doors in 2009 when the last staff left the site and took up posts elsewhere. Since then the site has remained empty and is beginning to decay. The hospital, its staff and the events that took place there mark an important chapter in the United Kingdom's medical and wartime history.

We started the day's shooting in the entrance arcade, its flagstone floors and tramway tracks still visible down the centre of the vaulted space. In this part of the building you get a real sense of just how old it is.

Leading off either side of the arcade, the hospital continues into modernised wards, offices, specialist areas and surgery suites, all stripped of equipment and beds. The vast interior of the building is a confusing warren and it took a good deal of the day to get our bearings as we moved about. There were some real stand-out sections, including a stunning oval staircase that accessed all floors; the original basement areas which doubled as operating suites during war time; a blood testing department still littered with glass vials and a centrifuge; and endless corridors.

More than anything it was a great building to explore. New discoveries could continually be made. In fact, since returning, we have realised that we could easily spend another full day there and discover many new things.

Patients were brought inside the building on trams through large doors that lead into this arcade. One of the oldest parts of the hospital.

Bedside services panel.

Centrifuge in blood testing dept.

Mortuary slab.

Exterior view of the hospital.

The Grade II listed Water Tower.

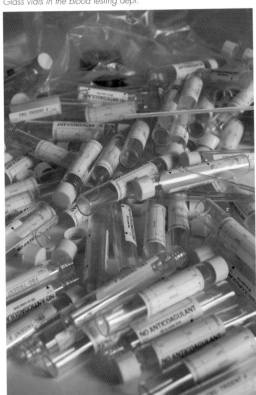

Looking straight up through the spiral staircase.

Another view inside
the entrance arcade.
One of the remaining
tram tracks can be seen
in the stone floor.

One of the deserted corridors in the newer part of the hospital, near to the surgical suites.

Abandoned Power Station

Belgium

Next is a large Belgian coal and natural gas-fuelled power plant that was closed in 2013 after 54 years of service; its closure was down to the fact it was no longer profitable and it produced the highest CO_2 emissions in the country. An increase in renewable energy and high CO_2 emissions at coal plants are one of the main reasons Europe's power stations are being closed down.

Our first view of the plant was impressive. As we drove over the crest of a hill along one of the country's dual carriageways, below us a large river meandered its way across the wide valley floor. On its banks the vast power plant stretched skywards: chimneys, conveyor systems, storage silos, huge sheds and in the centre of it all, one of the biggest cooling towers I had ever seen. The codename the site had been given was well chosen: welcome to 'Powerplant XL'.

An open space in the center of the main turbine hall. The doors on the first floor in the background lead into the main control room.

Parking well away from the site, we loaded up and walked along a road surrounded by fields of corn, heading for the site's remote south-eastern corner. After finding and climbing the fence we slowed our approach, keeping to the many bushes and trees that lined a track leading to the plant. We had heard that the on-site security could be heavy handed so we did our utmost not to be seen. Eventually we reached a final line of cover, some tall reeds that lined the edge of a reservoir close to the cooling tower. Hidden from view, we scanned the open ground for any signs of movement. We settled on a point to head for at the base of the tower and decided to go one at a time.

I broke cover and dashed across the dusty ground between two large silos, my heart racing and adrenaline pumping. On nearing the tower I realised that I could not get to it without first negotiating a gap in some security fencing. After a lot of squeezing and wriggling I ended up stuck, hung up by my bulky camera backpack. I looked back to see my two companions shaking their heads in despair. We quickly made our way under the base of the tower, finding a narrow crawl space between some vertical slats to access the interior. The site was totally silent but the wind racing through the slats around the tower made a constant high-speed clicking sound. Cooling towers have a strange effect, their sensory qualities fill me with awe; a feeling of space while still enclosed, converging walls leading to the opening far above inducing a kind of reverse vertigo. In short I felt photographically inspired the moment I stepped foot inside. We spent an hour or so here shooting several time-consuming vertical panoramas.

The wider site had been totally silent but once we moved inside the tower the sound of the wind racing through some of the loose slats around its base created an almost constant high-speed rattling sound. Once we were finished in the tower we made our way into the main power station building, another short dash across open ground on the far side of the tower. The way in led us through a very dark section of the ground floor filled with a multitude of valves and pipe work. Using our head torches to find a way through the metallic tangle, we emerged into a vast, brightly lit open hall stretching away into the distance. At ground level were rows of boilers and condensers. Above them on several platforms were the huge turbines that had generated the electrical output of the plant. Scattered throughout were panels containing controls, dials and gauges. The sheer scale and the complexity of the technologies contained within never cease to amaze. (For me it's the idea that when we do something simple like flick a light switch at home, behind that simple action lies such a complex industrial process. It is clear that our energy needs are fast approaching a crunch time, so visiting a plant like this brings home the scale of the problems we face in terms of cost and infrastructure.)

We spent a further few hours exploring the vast space from the ground floor up, eventually emerging onto gantries that ran around the rolling crane carriages far above the turbine hall floor. No doubt the plant's staff all wore safety harnesses when working up there, so getting shots without one required us to pay extra attention to every move we made.

We spent a good four hours exploring the site and came away with some great images and new perspectives on the energy industry.

The view along the main turbine hall from the platform of a rolling crane.

Pipework designed to
carry pressurised steam
around the plant.

The insides one of
the condensers on
the ground floor of
the plant. Its metal front
has been cut away to
deter metal thieves.

Control panel on the ground floor of the plant.

Rows of buttons and dials in the main control room.

One of the ways into
the interior of the large
cooling tower in
the center of the site.

The dizzying
internal space of
the sites large
cooling tower.

Ruined Chateau

Belgium

Another truly breathtaking and historic location that stays in the memory long after your visit. This gloriously impressive ruin is hidden away in densely forested hills in a remote region of Belgium. Although still standing at the time of writing, there have been plans to demolish it for a considerable time, so it may no longer exist.

Having seen many images of this castle since the moment my interest in shooting abandoned heritage began, I knew I would end up there sooner or later. My moment came in Spring 2013 on a trip where, for once, only two of our regular group could make it across the channel. My companion had been to the castle previously and was an excellent guide on how to approach it.

After climbing the hill that ran alongside the estate, we branched off through the woods and quietly made our way along a small hunting trail through thick woodland undergrowth in the rough direction of the ruins. The undergrowth that now surrounds the site is so thick that the building can only been seen when it is quite close by. In the years since it was last occupied, the castle has built up quite a reputation, drawing in photographers, artists, historians, romantics, campers, vandals and Satanists, to name a few, from all around the world.

Historically, the chateau has had quite a varied past. It was originally built in 1866 as a second home for a local family whose descendants still live in a neighbouring chateau. The castle was designed by the English architect Edward Milner, who died before completion of the build. The project was taken over by a French architect, Pelchner, who oversaw its completion in 1907. The family used the new chateau as a summer residence until the outbreak of the Second World War.

During the latter stages of the war this region experienced one of the most deadly battles of the whole conflict, 'The Battle of the Bulge'. On Christmas Day and Boxing Day, 1944, a battle between Allied Forces (US/English) and German armoured divisions took place one mile north of the chateau. The battle was ultimately won by the Allied Forces, but a detachment of German troops remained stationed at the chateau. It was around this time that fighting to liberate the castle broke out within its grounds.

After the war the family moved back into one of the wings of the castle. In 1958, the rest of the property was let out to the 'SNCB National Railway Company of Belgium', who used it as an orphanage and holiday camp for sickly children of company staff. At its height, the chateau housed around 200 children from Belgium, Holland and Italy. Education was provided on site and the fountain pond at the rear was even converted into a swimming pool. The treatment they received was often very successful; the all-female staff providing a variety of therapy, exercise, education and good food in the clean mountain air. The castle continued hosting the children until 1977, when the costs involved in the upkeep of the chateau became too great. It spent some time after that as a school and centre for seminars before finally closing for good in 1991.

Since this time the chateau has been at the mercy of the elements: the owner has on several occasions tried to find investors to bring the chateau back into use, but the costs involved have proved prohibitive and it has now moved beyond the realms of being realistically salvageable. Due to the site becoming dangerous to its almost daily influx of explorers, the owner has requested permission to demolish the castle. The risk to health and safety has prompted the Belgian authorities to reject the building for special protection from demolition and it now seems possible it may come down this year.

As we continued through the trees we passed a low raised enclosure. Overgrown with brambles and ferns and flanked by stone corner posts - it looked like it might have been a private cemetery. A short distance ahead of this first clue, the woods seemed noticeably darker and after another few dozen steps the solid bulk of a stone wall could be made out among the thick trees and bushes. This was my first sight of the castle structure. It emerged from the woods like a lost temple materialising from the jungle. This feeling of 'discovery' added an element of magic to our visit.

We approached a set of side buildings, which included the stable block, and these were in a very bad state. The roof had completely collapsed after a bad storm in 2006 and everything was in a bad state. Making our way around them, we emerged into the rear gardens area looking for a way into the main building. Many of the windows were just empty frames and after a quick up and over we were in.

Once inside, the castle did not disappoint. Though in a severe state of decay, its impressive architectural features could still be made out. It had once been such a majestic building and standing within, surrounded by such beauty reduced to chaos and rubble, gave us chills. Exploring the interior proved to be a tricky endeavour - it was still a fairly dangerous place to be. Many of the upper floors had collapsed after being weakened by rain. Where floors remained there were many holes. And certain corridors were simply no-go areas.

Despite the obstacles the interior had many ways to reach the various wings. Certain parts required you to go down a set of stairs, traverse part of that floor then go back up another staircase; by using this technique you could access parts of the building that at first seemed like they might have been cut off by a collapse. Dotted throughout the western wings there were signs of the schooling that took place here; bathrooms with long rows of low mounted washbasins, classrooms with large chalkboards still on the wall and large walk-in baths. But other than occasional signs of previous use, the castle was fairly well stripped and most rooms were nothing more than empty, decaying shells.

Having explored as much of the interior as we felt we could without putting ourselves in too much danger, we headed outside – another one of the golden rules, and for fairly obvious reasons, is to leave the exterior shots until last. The open ground in front of the chateau provides some iconic imagery with it's 56 meter high central tower and Neo-Gothic styling. Feeling inspired by such incredible beauty we worked at capturing images of the building's stunning frontage before heading back to the car.

Warning: The chateau is in an advanced state of decay and is potentially a very dangerous place to explore. Visiting is not advised.

Abandoned Coke Works
Wales, UK

This was originally the site of a colliery that opened in 1909; it operated two shafts (Margaret and Mildred) at a depth of 685 metres. In 1947 the UK's coal industry was nationalised and the National Coal Board (NCB) took over the running of the plant. The NCB immediately went about adding a coking plant to supply the nearby foundries at Port Talbot with coke for use in their blast furnaces. In 1986 the coal industry was sold off to private enterprise and CPL Industries, who took up the reins, ceased all mining activity to focus purely on coke production. The plant ran for a further 16 years until it became outdated, finally closing in 2002. It has sat empty since then and is one of Wales largest derelict industrial sites.

*The flooded
basement below
the coke ovens.*

The coke works is a well-known location that had been on our radar for quite some time. In 2014, in poor weather, we paid it a short visit. Exploring the site felt pretty dangerous; there is rusting metal everywhere, basement areas are often flooded with water covered in a prismatic layer of oils and chemicals, rusty pipes hang down at head height and walkways are often missing guardrails. In short, the advanced state of decay means the site is an accident waiting to happen.

Many visitors climb staircases or follow covered coal belt systems upwards into the highest parts of the site. But despite the views that can be gained, we stayed at ground level. All sites carry a degree of risk, but with a bit of common sense and care, those risks can be substantially reduced. At this location safety felt more like a roll of the dice.

The site is spread over a large area, much of it covered in thick foliage. That, combined with boggy, waterlogged ground, made moving around quite tricky. We entered in the northernmost section near a row of terraced houses. Very shortly after going over the fence we heard some shouting nearby and saw a figure moving along the fence line. We stopped and waited for a few minutes inside a small building. When we emerged the figure had moved on. Local people can often be fiercely protective of abandoned locations; the site is no doubt popular with metal thieves and I guess it comes down to the fact that residents don't want criminal elements lingering close to where they live.

Aware that security could be patrolling, we moved south through the many outbuildings towards the centre of the site and the imposing concrete structure that housed the coke ovens. We soon realised that the foliage growing from the roads was a sure sign that vehicles no longer drove the site. Security had likely not been present here for some time.

We made our way inside the long, tall structure. Directly below the main coke ovens we discovered an almost endless row of what looked like boilers. It was dark and tight inside, punctuated by gaps allowing access down a ladder into a flooded basement area. Everything in the damp gloom below was covered in a layer of grime – quite an unpleasant environment. After climbing up from the basement and continuing along the rows of rusting boilers, we came across a collection of ferns growing right on top of one. A small side window provided just enough light and the humidity was obviously high enough for this tiny spark of life to take hold in such inhospitable surroundings. This battle between man's creations and nature is a repeating theme across all the locations I photograph. Nature patiently waits until our back is turned before stepping in to reclaim and recycle the land. Given time, even the mightiest structures will succumb and crumble.

Leaving the coke ovens behind, we explored the southern end of the site, but the constant rain eventually forced us to head back to the car. On the way back, we spotted a scene that would have made a great shot. But we were keen to get out of the wet and passed by instead, giving us a reason to return here in the future.

A small spark of life takes hold in a lifeless environment.

Following page: Part of the industrial landscape in the center of the huge industrial complex.

Box and Spring Quarries
Wiltshire, UK

Deep below the town of Corsham and surrounding villages in Wiltshire lies a vast network of tunnels and chambers. These subterranean spaces have been extensively quarried since 1844: six years after Isambard Kingdom Brunel drove the Box Railway Tunnel almost two miles through Box Hill. During the boring of the tunnel, Brunel noted the large amounts of Great Oolite Limestone being brought out of the ground. Known locally as Bath Stone, Great Oolite has been used for centuries across South West England in construction projects.

A huge corridor sized fan in one of the air drifts in the militarised section of Spring Quarry.

Once the tunnel was completed, companies moved in and began extracting the valuable stone. The underground areas quickly expanded outwards from the original finds and further exploratory shafts were sunk into the ground in the search for further deposits. The first of the major quarries took shape just to the north and was named Tunnel Quarry. A branch line joined the quarry through a separate entrance adjacent to the eastern end of Box Tunnel and terminated underground at a half-mile long platform where the stone could be loaded directly onto trains.

In 1875 work began on Spring Quarry to the south of the railway tunnel. In time it would become the second largest of the quarries after Tunnel Quarry.

As work continued, the underground spaces began joining up. In total, the contiguous underground area eventually included the following quarries: Box Freestone Quarry, Groundstone Quarry, Browns Quarry, Tunnel Quarry, Thorney Pits, Sands Quarry and Spring Quarry with its huge East and West Lung sections. The underground contained hundreds of kilometres of passages stretching 2.5km east to west and 1.5km north to south.

By the early part of the 20th Century a huge amount of Bath Stone had been extracted and many of the quarries had closed down; the underground became dark and still. Then in 1940 the Luftwaffe bombed the nearby Bristol Aeroplane Company, which was vital to the war effort. The government looked to the quarries as a way of protecting the expensive manufacturing of munitions, tank and aeroplane parts. Throughout the remainder of the war many of the quarries were converted for military use; rough floors were flattened and paved, walls and ceilings were strengthened with steel supports and additional ventilation was created for the thousands of workers below ground.

Tunnel Quarry became one of several Central Ammunition Depots, Spring Quarry a factory for the production of aeroplane parts and Browns Quarry became a headquarters for RAF Command, all safe from the bombing above. Once the war was over the factories were closed down, but the government, keen to maximise its investment, kept the quarries on as storage areas.

As relations with the USSR deteriorated during the Cold War, the Conservative government requisitioned a sizeable area of the northern section of Spring Quarry for use as a nuclear relocation shelter. It was built under extreme secrecy so as not to alert the Russians to its location. Even Whitehall officials who were 'on the list' to relocate in the event of an attack were not made aware of its existence. The underground platform in Tunnel Quarry would have been used to receive passengers direct from London. The completed bunker (codenamed Burlington) included canteens, laundries, barracks, dormitories, workshops, a power plant, various offices for the military, an armoury, a government war room and staff areas, an underground lake of drinking water, a large telephone exchange and over 80 kilometres of paved roads. The bunker was designed to house around 4000 people for up to two months; it was a place where the establishment could survive the initial attack while planning to rebuild what was left of the towns, cities and society above. But the attack never came and the Cold War gradually warmed to the point that this huge, fully stocked, underground city became redundant. By the early 1990s most of the maintenance staff had left and by 1994 the site was declassified – what many local people had long suspected about the strange goings on in the area had finally been confirmed.

A dismantled fan housing on the outer edge of the Burlington Bunker. The top secret and fortunately never used nuclear shelter for government staff during The Cold War.

Today the underground areas are still largely owned by the MOD or rented by private enterprise. At ground level, above the now derelict bunker, MOD Corsham has been developed into an important military headquarters and the only entrances to the bunker fall within the perimeter of the base. The old underground entrances from the publicly accessible parts of the quarries were either sealed up with solid cement caps many years ago or lie locked behind heavy metal doors.

For the exploring/photographic community and indeed many other interested groups, the bunker, its contents and its important place in Cold War history exude a magnetism akin to that of a fabled lost city. People are obsessed with wanting to see inside. I think it has a lot to do with the innate lure of the forbidden.

I first became aware of the quarries back in 2010. I caught an image online of a person standing in The Cathedral, on a rubble-strewn slope within a tall rocky chamber, stretching upwards to a hole in the roof where daylight streamed in. The picture was so striking that it stuck in my memory. I saw it again a few more times and with each viewing I thought to myself 'I will find out where this is and go there one day'. This is something I love about photography as a hobby; it forces you into the role of a hunter, gets you out of your home and into the world, seeking out the imagery that is your prey. Eventually I learned its name, 'Box Freestone Quarry'. From there it was only a short time before we got the chance to visit.

Woefully unprepared for this first short journey, we acquired the key from a local pub and unlocked the gate that formed a barrier to the labyrinth of passages ahead. The first set of chambers were strewn with large boulders that had fallen from the roof over time. We picked our way methodically from boulder to boulder to avoid slipping and falling. Before long we encountered a narrow rift that allowed passage by climbing up into the tight gap and squeezing sideways for around 3 metres. Once on the other side, the continuation of passages settled into a more regular rhythm of multiple-choice junctions followed by short sections of passages leading to even more junctions. It was complex and, with no landmarks to tell which way was which, it was clear that coming down here without any navigational aids was a dangerous risk to have taken. We considered turning back, but knowing that The Cathedral was not far we pushed on, hoping that we would be able to find our way out again.

After travelling for fifteen minutes through angular, rock-strewn passageways, we started noticing a 'Cath' marking with an arrow sprayed on the walls at each junction. Following them through a few more junctions we saw up ahead a pool of light on the floor. We quickened our pace and emerged into the photograph I had seen many years before. It felt like a pilgrimage of sorts, placing another tick against my long and steadily growing bucket list of amazing places to see and photograph.

On this day we went no further and made our way back through the same junctions. There was only a short hiccup where we seemed to get momentarily lost before recognising a large slab of rock in the centre of a passage that led us to the narrow gap we had squeezed through on the way in.

Naval part storage racks within a disused section of Spring quarry.

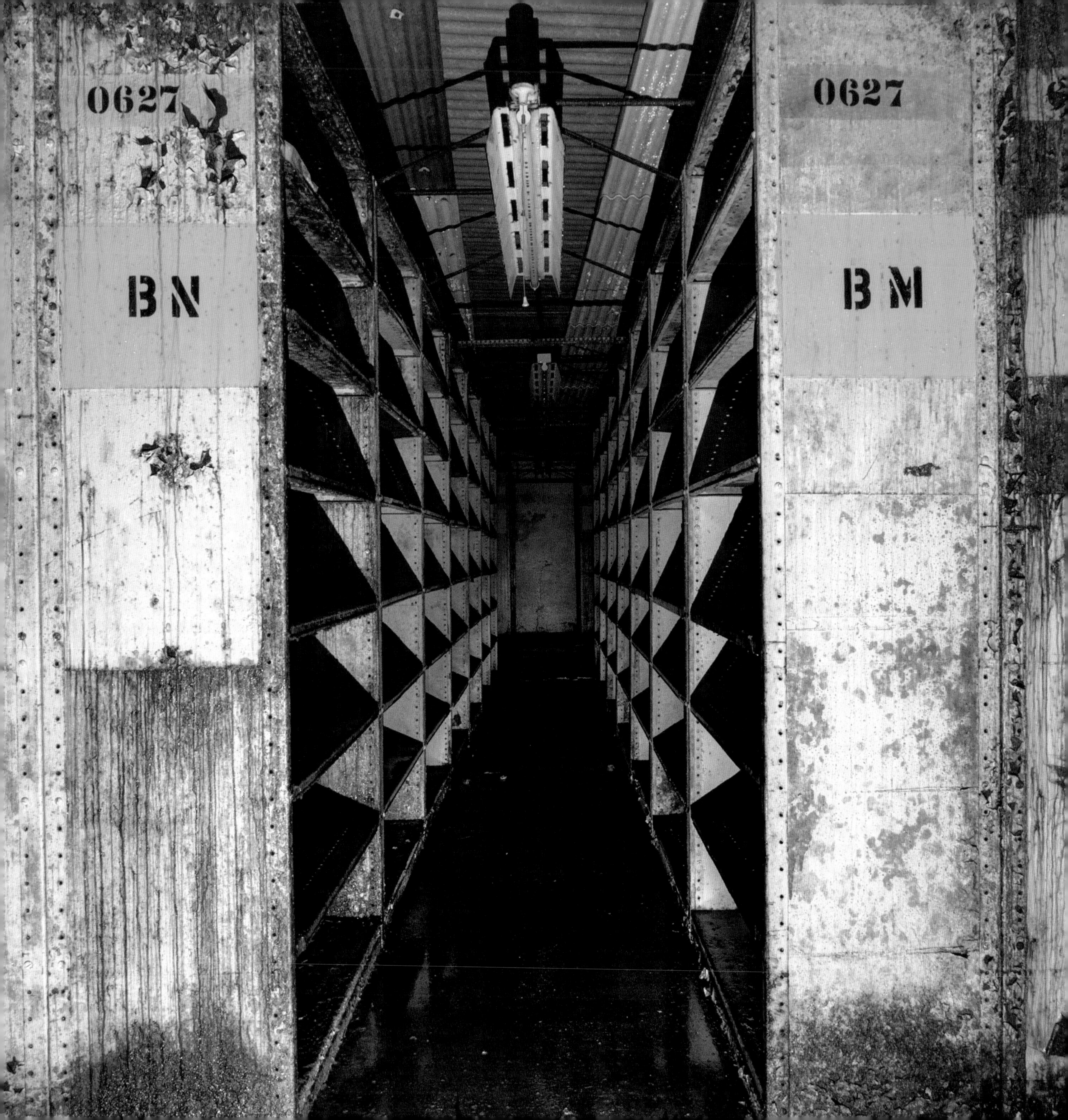
0627
BN
0627
BM

Numerous trips followed and we pushed further and further into the maze of passageways. Our aim was to reach the borders of the military-owned areas. We used a better navigational method in the form of laminated squares of card with arrows drawn on them. At every new junction we placed an arrow on the ground pointing back at the previous junction. When it was time to make our way back out we simply followed the arrows, picking them up as we went. It worked incredibly well.

On the third trip, a considerable distance into the quarry, we found what we had been looking for: a large side passage blocked by a huge steel grille that was adorned with coils of barbed wire and signs declaring 'MOD property – access strictly prohibited'. Someone had cut through a section of the grille, enabling us to climb through and make our way along a large passage known as Brewers Drift. This marked our first transition from Box Quarry into one of the neighbouring quarries, 'Brownstone'.

After several hundred metres, we approached a walled-off section with a heavy metal door set into it. Constant whooshing and humming sounds could be heard just beyond the door – a large ventilation fan running inside the military-owned Tunnel Quarry. To be this close (just 50 metres or so beyond the door) to the old government nuclear shelter was frustrating and exciting all at once. Just a few years earlier, an Oxford University and English Heritage survey had been carried out inside the bunker and for a short while this door had been left open. Word quickly spread that the bunker was accessible from below ground and a stream of photographers travelled here to spend entire nights exploring Burlington or '3 Site' as it was also known.

On a later visit, after an invite from a member of staff working at a data storage centre that was about to set up its operations in Spring Quarry, we did actually make it inside the military areas to the south of the bunker. We spent a day shooting the disused areas that served as the aircraft production factory during WWII. After the war the Admiralty used Spring Quarry as a storage area for naval engine parts and we got some shots of the racking that still remains, slowly rusting away. However, the star attractions were the large fans used to ventilate the subterranean network; there are numerous fans connected by long tunnels that kept the air flowing around the facility. Again, being just to the south of Burlington was tantalisingly close, but though it looked identical in many respects, it simply wasn't the fabled ground of the bunker itself. At one point we were a short crawl from it (a matter of 10 metres), beneath the blades of a stationary fan. But we were being monitored by a member of security as we photographed so all we could do was look at how close we were and wish we had been on our own. I imagine that will be the closest I ever get to making it inside; since the upgrading of MOD Corsham above, the site has become very secure. The days of being able to just walk in are long gone and trespassing on a site such as this would not be dealt with by a simple telling-off, which is a real shame because there is so much history down there, slowly rotting away a little more each year. Soon it will be gone.

Standing in the huge chamber known as 'The Cathedral' in Box Quarry.

Above ground the Wiltshire countryside is gorgeous.

Another viewpoint
on *The Cathedral*
in Box Quarry.

A large shutter in front of a ventilation fan, designed to close in the event of a gas attack above ground.

The boundaries between Box Quarry and the military sections below ground are marked by various security measures.

Inside, Spring quarry is paved and features many miles of roadways. A leftover from when it was an ammunition factory and storage area during the war.

MINISTRY OF DEFENCE

DANGER

DALEKS AND NINJAS
AND PIRATES AND SHIT!

*The famous locked red
door at the end of
Brownstone Quarry.
Beyond the door military
use is ongoing.*

Blast Furnaces

Belgium

Since the closing years of the last millennium, steel production in Europe has been in trouble. Production is not a clean process and new laws connected to climate change have been implemented to reduce the amount of CO_2 produced, adding further costs; steel production uses huge amounts of power and the rising cost of energy in Europe has put further financial strain on the industry; the price of raw materials is rising; demand from industries that buy steel has gone down but one of the biggest issues faced is the low price of steel imported from countries such as China, where production costs are much lower and the amount of steel produced is huge. This global market saturation devalues the product and many European plants can now only sell steel for less than it costs to produce.

Furthermore, in the interests of fair competition, the European Union places a block on governments subsidising industry, while countries outside the EU are free to subsidise, thus creating a decidedly unlevel playing field.

The main core of the second furnace we visited. Most of the Tuyere injectors have been removed and the un-smelted iron ore and coke can be seen just inside.

As a result, many plants around Europe have been forced to close, the loss of thousands of jobs often decimating long-standing communities, even entire towns, in the process. However, steel is a cornerstone of modern civilisation; infrastructure, transportation, shipping and all kinds of construction projects depend upon it. Without steel, the world as we know it simply would not exist.

In one of Belgium's larger industrial cities, along the banks of a large river, lies a series of blast furnaces that have been closed for only a few years. Covering vast tracts of land along the riverbank, they dominate the skyline with towers of rusting metal, gantries, pipes and conveyor systems. To some, the presence of heavy industry is nothing more than an eyesore, representative only of the past. In the context of steel's vital importance to modern society, I see those 'eyesores' as the symbolic hearts of urban centres such as this, the waterways that brought in the raw materials on barges, the arteries. In their own way they have a strange kind of beauty – impressive structures of massive scale, commanding awe and respect for their roles in shaping our modern way of life.

We visited two of these abandoned plants in 2014 and 2015. The first visit was to furnace number 6, occupying about a third of a partially decommissioned site. We crept silently through a rail yard one late afternoon and up an embankment that ran alongside the furnace. We passed beneath pipes that carried rushing water; in other areas steam vented from valves in a loud and sudden hiss. Being an active site, we were aware that getting caught here could be problematic, so doubts entered our minds. We agreed that I would continue into the site and check it out while my companion waited at the embankment – if I thought it worthwhile, we would return first thing in the morning and spend a few hours there. After ten minutes of sneaking about, poking my head in doors and sprinting up stairs to the main blast furnace platform, I returned with the news that it would most definitely be worth it.

Arriving at dawn, we were soon inside and setting up around the base of the tower. In simple terms, a blast furnace is a tall vertical chamber with conveyor systems feeding a constant supply of raw materials into the neck (top) of the furnace. The raw materials consist of alternating layers of coke over iron sinter pellets and limestone. A blast of hot (1200 degrees) air is pumped into the base of the furnace through a ring of injectors called 'tuyeres'. The mix of raw materials in the lower part of the furnace becomes molten as the coke combusts at temperatures reaching 1600 degrees. As the coke burns along with the oxygen it releases carbon monoxide, helping convert the iron ore into iron. The limestone combines with impurities in the coke and iron ore, which is skimmed off as slag before the remaining molten pig iron is tapped at the base of the tower. The molten metal is then transported to the furnace where the pig iron is converted into pure steel.

Standing where we had set up our tripods would have been impossible during the smelting process – the full length asbestos suits and face masks hanging nearby were testament to the insane temperatures that radiate from an active furnace.

The central core is covered in a profusion of pipes that snake in all directions seemingly at random, generating wonderful imagery. Industry always provides such a thrill for a photographer; the scenes presented are like nothing seen before, making it so much easier to capture compelling imagery.

There is complex pipe work everywhere close to the main furnace.

Moving out from the furnace is a series of other structures. We investigated further and discovered what would have been a staff changing area and administration building. The interior was bare and damp with ferns growing from gaps in the concrete floor. A room full of lockers toppled against each other like dominos. It's amazing how in just a handful of years a location can progress so far along its journey into chaos.

The following year we came in a group of four to visit furnace B a few kilometres along the river. This site is much larger and includes within its borders the processing facilities for the raw materials. Exploring it for the four hours we had allotted just about allowed us to the scratch the surface, leaving us plenty of scope for future visits.

Entering via a section of wall where the razor wire was missing, we walked silently in single file along walkways that were slowly being swallowed by undergrowth, past huge open sheds with corrugated sheeting flapping and clanging in the wind. We emerged from the myriad metal structures onto one of the main roads that ran through the site, looking both ways for signs of any security. However, it was early and the site was still and quiet. We made our way along ground level tracks to the centre and climbed the steps to the platform surrounding the furnace. Although slightly different from furnace 6, the basic layout was similar, although this time some of the tuyeres around the base were missing, leaving holes leading to the interior. After crawling through onto the pile of coke and iron ore that still remained, I twisted and looked up; the view to the top was breathtaking and I would have loved to have captured an 'up' shot. However, I noticed the inner walls of the furnace were lined with rows of blocks made from an unknown material.

Wary that it could be asbestos, I was quickly outside again. Since returning from the trip and speaking to a friend that works at a steel plant, I have discovered that they were simply heat resistant bricks. Taking the shot would have been quite safe; that's one for next time.

The sudden noise of a car engine close by snapped us quickly to attention. Heart rates quickened, tripods were hastily gathered and bags zipped up. The car passed directly below us. Clutching our gear, ready to run for cover, we waited for it to stop. But the sound faded into the distance. The car drove the site throughout the rest of the morning, but the lone driver never stopped to investigate anything above ground level. Despite the security presence, moving around the site was still reasonably risk free thanks to the many raised conveyor systems that once carried raw materials to the furnace from the processing factories on the peripheries. When it was time to leave and move onto the second location of the day, we used them to make our way back to our exit point.

A view of the main furnace from an upper gantry at the second plant.

A corridor in a staff
building at the first of
the wto furnaces.

The Tuyere injectors were still in place at the first furnace.

Ferns grow in
a corner of
a large staff area
at furnace 6.

A walkway near
to furnace 6.

Conveyor systems that carried the raw materials to the top of the furnace for smelting to take place.

A shot of a small detail at the first furnace site.

Pipes cling to the exterior of the first furnace.

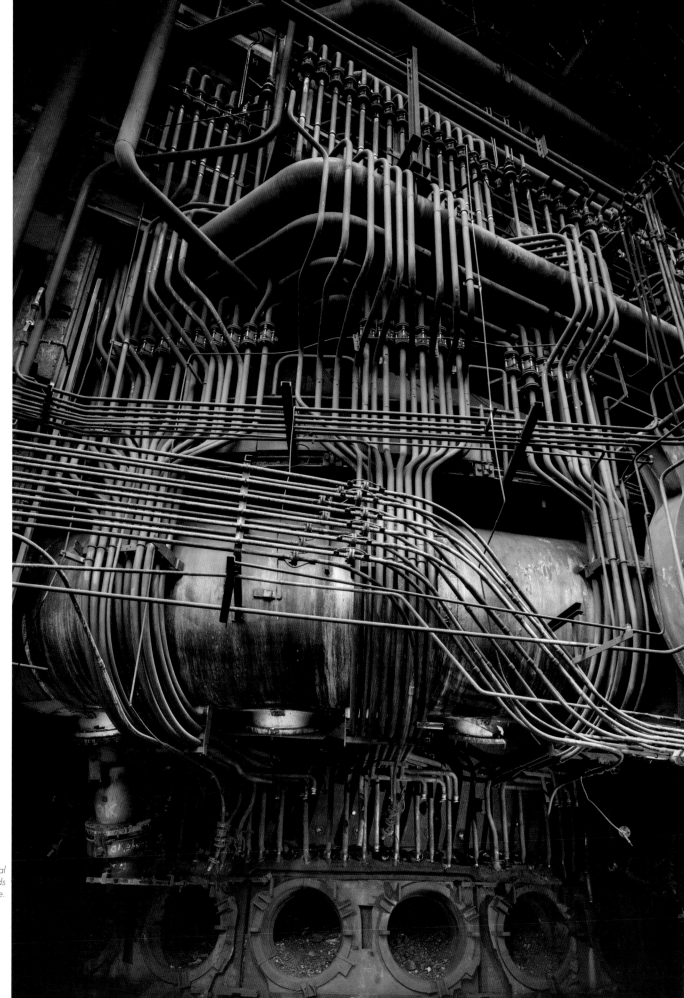

The complex metal work that surrounds the second furnace.

The control desk for controlling the tap hole robot arm at blast furnace B.

Acknowledgements

The field of abandoned photography is becoming more and more popular with each passing year and I think it ceased inhabiting its photographic niche a few years ago. However, when compared with oversubscribed fields like landscape, nature or portraiture, it still couldn't be classed as mass market. It is also a field that is blessed with highly skilled photographers. When I first started out, I was amazed and inspired by the work of many people: the tangible mood instilled into the images of Rebecca Bathory, the masterful photography and post-processing work of Andre Govia, the "standing within the picture" realism in Rez*'s industrial landscapes, Jeremy Gibbs' high-art model shoots among the ruins or the painterly quality of Gina Soden's photographic art. The approach to capturing abandonment from these and the many other photographers I admire is as varied as it is brilliant. Thank you to so many photographers for producing such inspiring work.

The wider community is made up not just of photographers but a whole gamut of interest groups who are fascinated by these places for many reasons. What stands out is the genuine respect and passion shown towards the locations by the people I have met. Over the last four years, I have learned a great deal about the history of the buildings, been given photographic advice and gained some good friends. I thank all of you for being on this journey with me and extending the hand of friendship.

I travel to photograph these places with a small group of great people who, besides being gifted photographers themselves, are fantastic companions on these trips. I am always amazed at just how differently we all interpret each location through our images. Mark, Darren, Lex and Jeremy: thanks for all the great adventures and the fun times we have shared. I look excitedly to the future.

Without the support of so many people following my work on social media, this book most certainly would not have been possible. All of you who take the time to share your thoughts and passion for the images I post have made it all worthwhile and indeed a lot of fun. Keep up the good work and I hope you enjoy this book.

Some great companies have supported me by supplying the equipment I use to capture these images. Rolf at Scurion: your amazing lights have been invaluable in lighting up the dark places. Mark at Pentax: your cameras have produced the goods time and again and the loan of the 645Z blew my mind; the last two years have been a blast. Sarah at Manfrotto: the tripod, head and bag will be of great service going forward. I thank you all for your generosity and support.

Thanks to Thomas and the team at Jonglez. Your understanding when things got tough was appreciated and you provided great assistance during the production process. Thanks for putting your trust in me.

Thanks to you, Paula, for all the help you provided in editing the copy with me and making sure my grammar got corrected; you have been a star. Who said mothers-in-law were hard work?

Thanks to my father, who bought me my first camera and taught me how to use it. You have always been an inspiration to me through your thirst for knowledge and mastery of skills. Nothing but love and appreciation for who you are and what you have done for me.

My family have endured a lot whilst I created this book and photographed these locations over the last four years. As the book's deadline approached, they saw less and less of me. Thank you to Melissa, Ben and Finn for putting up with it all. I promise I will now be a present and engaged partner and father. Without your huge love and support I would not have been able to do this.

Lastly I would like to dedicate this book to the memory of my mother, Doreen Susan Emmett. She was diagnosed with cancer early on in the writing process and died before I could complete the book. I know how proud she was of me and I hope in some way this book can be a tribute to her kindness and the love she poured into our family every day. She will always be in my thoughts. Thank you, Mum.

Bibliography

Chapter – National Gas Turbine Establishment:

Cornwell, S. (2007 – 2015). "Welcome to Pyestock" (online) available at: http://www.ngte.co.uk/ (accessed June 15, 2016).

Knight, M. (2007). "Pyestock" (online) available at: http://hotten.net/open/pages/indices/knight/ngte.htm (accessed June 15, 2016).

Chapter – Abandoned Ethanol Distillery:

Modica, M. (2009). "Eridania distilleria di Ferrara" (online) available at: http://www.st-al.com/archive/eridania_ferrara/scheda.html (accessed July 8, 2016).

Chapter – Abandoned Psychiatric Hospital:

Bello, D. (2007). "Ospedale neuropsichiatrico per la provincial di cuneo in racconigi" (online) available at: http://www.cartedalegare.san.beniculturali.it/fileadmin/redazione/inventari/Racconigi_OspedaleNeuropsichiatrico.pdf (accessed July 8, 2016).

Hutton & Fleming (1941). "Early results of prefrontal leucotomy" (online) available at: http://thirdworld.nl/early-results-of-prefrontal-leucotomy (accessed July 15, 2016).

All Things Considered (2005). "My Lobotomy: Howard Dully's Journey" (online) available at: http://www.npr.org/programs/all-things-considered/2005/11/16/12944948/ (accessed July 15, 2016).

Chapter – The Farm School:

Duseigne, V. (2012). "The Vocational School" (online) available at: http://tchorski.morkitu.org/9/waterloo-01.htm (accessed June 15, 2016).

JCX.BE (2016). "Bella Vita" (online) available at: http://www.jcx.be/sites/default/files/fiche_bella_vita_en_0.pdf (accessed June 15, 2016).

Chapter – Abandoned Power Station and Steel Plant:

Centre for European Studies and Research Robert Schuman, V. (2012). "Histoire de la sidérurgie Luxembourgeoise" (online) available at: http://www.cere.public.lu/fr/actualites/2012/05/Vient-d-etre-mis-en-ligne/Terres-rouges-histoire-de-la-siderurgie-luxembourgeoise_-_volume_1.pdf (Accessed July 16, 2016).

Encyclopedia.com (2006). "Arbed S.A." (online) available at: http://www.encyclopedia.com/topic/ARBED_S.A.aspx (accessed July 16, 2016).

Chapter – Royal Aircraft Establishment:

Historic England (2003). "Building R52 at Former Royal Aircraft Establishment Site" (online) available at: https://historicengland.org.uk/listing/the-list/list-entry/1390502 (accessed July 10, 2016).

Historic England (2003). "Building Q121 at Former Royal Aircraft Establishment Site" (online) available at: https://www.historicengland.org.uk/listing/the-list/list-entry/1259589 (accessed July 10, 2016).

Chapter – Colin's Barn:

Edmonds, L. (2013). "'I got a bit carried away': Sheep farmer spent 11 years building elaborate Hobbit House by hand - then abandoned it when a new quarry disturbed his peace" (online) available at: http://www.dailymail.co.uk/news/article-2492370/I-got-bit-carried-away-Sheep-farmer-spent-11-years-building-elaborate-Hobbit-House-hand--abandoned-new-quarry-disturbed-peace.html (accessed July 10, 2016).

Chapter – Abandoned Educational Institute:

Tomsin, P. (2009). "Carnets du Patrimoine – Montefiore Electrical Institute" (online) available at: https://www.ulg.ac.be/cms/c_155124/en/carnets-du-patrimoine-l-institut-electrotechnique-montefiore (accessed June 20, 2016).

Chapter – Ruined Gwrych Castle:

Wikipedia (2016). "Gwrych Castle" (online) available at: https://en.wikipedia.org/wiki/Gwrych_Castle (accessed May 13, 2016).

Gwrych Trust (2016). "The History of Gwrych Castle" (online) available at: http://gwrychtrust.co.uk/index.php/history/ (accessed May 13, 2016).

Chapter – Abandoned Tool Makers Factory:

Rippner, D. (2016). *Leathersmithe* (online) available at: http://www.leathersmithe.com/archive/barnsley–sons-toolmakers–.html (accessed July 5, 2016).

Chapter – Country Estate Ruins:

Wikipedia (2016). "Baron Hill House" (online) available at: https://en.wikipedia.org/wiki/Baron_Hill_(house) (accessed May 20, 2016).

Chapter – Satellite Communication Station:

Joosse, A. (2014). "Navo Satcom F1" (online) available at: http://www.urbex.nl/site/navo-satcom-f1/ (accessed July 10, 2016).

Colpaert, M. (2014). "Werken Satcom gaan van start" (online) available at: http://www.hln.be/regio/nieuws-uit-gooik/werken-satcom-gaan-van-start-a1884785/ (accessed July 10, 2016).

Chapter – Abandoned Textile Mill:

Wikipedia (2016). "Fox Brothers" (online) available at: https://en.wikipedia.org/wiki/Fox_Brothers (accessed June 18, 2016).

Wikipedia (2016). "Tonedale Mills" (online) available at: https://en.wikipedia.org/wiki/Tonedale_Mills (accessed June 18, 2016).

Chapter – Royal Hospital Haslar:

Birback, E. (2009). *Haslar Heritage Group* (online) available at: http://www.haslarheritagegroup.co.uk/ (accessed June 2, 2016).

BBC. (2014). "Historic Figures" (online) available at: http://www.bbc.co.uk/history/historic_figures/lind_james.shtml (accessed June 2, 2016).

Chapter – Ruined Chateau:

Baker, D. (2013). "The History of Chateau Noisy" (online) available at: http://www.davidbakerphotography.com/projects/residential/the-history-of-chateau-de-noisy-chateau-miranda-belgium (accessed April 21, 2016).

Morton, E. (2014). "The Remains of Chateau Miranda" (online) available at: http://www.slate.com/blogs/atlas_obscura/2014/09/29/abandoned_noisy_castle_or_miranda_castle_in_belgium.html (accessed April 21, 2016).

Chapter – Abandoned Coke Works:

Welsh Coal Mines (2010). "Cwm Beddau" (online) available at: http://www.welshcoalmines.co.uk/GlamEast/cwmbeddau.htm (accessed April 21, 2016).

Chapter – Box and Spring Quarries:

Nettleden.com (2016). "Various quarries" (online) available at: http://www.nettleden.com/venues/ (accessed April 21, 2016).

Wikipedia (2016). "Central Government War Headquarters" (online) available at: https://en.wikipedia.org/wiki/Central_Government_War_Headquarters (accessed July 4, 2016).

Higgins, S. (2016). "The Story of Burlington" (online) available at: http://www.burlingtonbunker.co.uk/history/ (accessed July 4, 2016).

Pollard, D. (2014). "Quarrying in Box after 1800" (online) available at: http://www.boxpeopleandplaces.co.uk/box-quarries.html (accessed July 4, 2016).

All photographs by Matt Emmett

Photo copyrights: Matt Emmett
Design: Stéphanie Benoit
Editing: Matt Gay
Proof-reading: Kimberly Bess

© **JONGLEZ 2016**
Registration of copyright: August 2016 – Edition: 01
ISBN: 978-2-36195-162-7
Printed in China by Toppan